Searching for Aunt Dot

Surprised by a Lutheran Woman's Story

Ann Wagner, Ph.D.
with Kimberly Tucker, M.Ed.
& Gary Wilkerson, Ph.D.

Foreword by President John Swallow
of Carthage College and
his wife, Cameron

Lutheran University Press
Minneapolis, Minnesota

Searching for Aunt Dot
Surprised by a Lutheran Woman's Story
by Ann Wagner
with Kimberly Tucker & Gary Wilkerson

Copyright 2019 Ann Wagner. All rights reserved. Published by Lutheran University Press, an imprint of 1517 Media. No part of this publication may be reproduced, stored in a retrieval system, or transmitted in any form or by any means, electronic, mechanical, photocopying, recording, or otherwise, without prior permission of the publisher.

ISBN 978-1-942304-34-0
eISBN 978-1-942304-76-0

Contents

Acknowledgments 5

Foreword 7
by Dr. John and Cameron Swallow

Introduction 9

CHAPTER ONE
Betrayed 13

CHAPTER TWO
Growing Up German, Lutheran, and Female 21

CHAPTER THREE
Choices 45

CHAPTER FOUR
A Wedding with Clouds in View 67

CHAPTER FIVE
Tracing an Army Chaplain's Wife 87

CHAPTER SIX
Desertion, Then Divorce 105

CHAPTER SEVEN
New Challenges 117

CHAPTER EIGHT
A Second Marriage with a Surprise Twist 137

Epilogue
    The Gift of Resilience 155
    by the Rev. Dr. Gary Wilkerson

    A Brief Guide to Research Strategies and Sources 172
    by Kimberly Tucker

About the Authors 185

Dorothy Louise Wagner (1913-1961), in an undated photo.

Acknowledgments

The following pages are a tale of research that comes to life in the form of a story, which began over a century ago. As the researcher and storyteller, I am grateful for the encouragement, comments and questions of two long-time friends. Kathy Wise, psychologist, and Regina Johnson, teacher, both believed in this project from the beginning. They gave of their time and talent in critically reading an earlier version of the manuscript.

Completed in 1918, Denhart Hall housed all of the women students on the Carthage College campus in Illinois.

Foreword

Searching for Aunt Dot: Surprised by a Lutheran Woman's Story is a narrative that works on multiple levels. First, it tells straightforwardly the story of a woman raised in a strong family of German Lutheran heritage in the American Midwest of the early twentieth century. Second, it illuminates the social landscape and the choices available to women as that landscape changed during and after the Second World War. Third and most movingly, it joins Dot's story to the story of her niece Ann, the author, who is investigating Dot's life in pursuit of greater understanding of her aunt, her family, and her own identity.

The fact that the stories of both aunt and niece intersect significantly the story of Carthage College adds an extra layer of fascination for those of us associated with the institution. Carthage contributed to the education and cultural formation of Dot, her brothers, and her first husband; it was committed to educating women alongside men before the twentieth century began, and its approach to education for women changed and grew as the landscape of that century changed and grew.

In writing this book Ann Wagner has sought to understand the facts of Dot's life, and she has had to do a good bit of sleuthing to uncover and corroborate those facts. In confronting the facts and reconstructing a narrative, Ann seeks the significance of Dot's story—of the situations in which Dot found herself, of the options that society and fate permitted Dot to consider, and of the choices she made within those contexts. And Ann succeeds, finding meaning in Dot's place in changing historical circumstances, particularly regarding gender roles and opportunities. She also succeeds in communicating Dot's essential character and imagination, designing and redesigning a life that she wanted, pursued, and could achieve. We are moved by Dot's story, and by Ann Wagner's story of her aunt and family. We know you will be moved as well.

Dr. John Swallow, 23rd President of Carthage College, and his wife, Cameron Swallow

Evergreen Walk connected the formal entrance to the College with Old Main, the first building on the Illinois campus, and commemorated in the college song:

> Looking far o'er Hancock Prairie
> Rising from the plain
> Monument to years of wisdom
> Stands our dear Old Main.

Introduction

Most stories have an identifiable beginning. This story began with *schnitzelbonen*.

During an infrequent phone chat a few years ago with my cousin Kate, who lives in Utah, she asked me if I had Grandma Wagner's recipe for *schnitzelbonen*. I didn't have to do a lengthy search in my recipe box to find it. Nevertheless, the process prompted me to think about writing our Wagner family history. My few cousins were scattered about the country and had never lived in Davenport, Iowa, where our grandparents spent their entire lives. Growing up in Rock Island, Illinois, directly across the Mississippi from Davenport, made me the logical candidate. That, combined with my love of history and being retired, prompted me to begin the story. At the outset, I intended just to research and write about our grandparents, their German immigrant ancestors, and our parents. But something happened to my consciousness along the way. I became acutely aware of the difficulties in researching Aunt Dot. She was a wife of several titles—wife-in-waiting, housewife, minister's wife, war wife. I also realized that she was the only one in this staunchly Lutheran family who had been divorced and remarried. In my mind that reality made her a quiet rebel and a very strong woman.

Insight, information, and perspective about Aunt Dot's older brothers and parents were relatively easy to discover. My cousins and I had personal knowledge of our fathers and their careers. We had some personal recollections of our grandparents as well as anecdotal history of them from our fathers. In addition, school records plus employment and military history were accessible. However, much of that information was absent for Aunt Dot. She had been a wife for most of her adult life and apparently lacked a career history outside her home. She had no children and left no letters or diaries. Moreover, she lived the last third of her life in Tampa, Florida. Yet, the few facts I knew about her piqued my curiosity.

When I began this search, here is what I knew about Aunt Dot: She died at the age of 48 after fighting breast cancer for the last few years of her life. She had taught deaf and hard-of-hearing children when she lived in Tampa, but I didn't know when, where, or for how long. Moreover, I had no idea why or when she had moved to Tampa. Her brothers' families all had remained in the Midwest. Aunt Dot had been divorced from her first husband, August Gruhn, a Lutheran pastor with German ethnic roots. I vaguely remembered hearing that Gruhn and Aunt Dot had met as students at Carthage College when it was located in Illinois. I thought that she had left college after two years in order to work in Minneapolis, where he probably had attended seminary, but I wasn't sure. My cousins and I knew John Zambon, her second husband. However, we only saw Aunt Dot and Uncle John during brief summer vacations when they came to visit our grandparents in Davenport, but it seemed clear to us that John Zambon was neither German nor Lutheran nor Midwestern. I also vaguely remembered my parents commenting that he did not have a college degree. So, when I began this search, I had to look for Aunt Dot's lost life.

To recreate Aunt Dot's early life, I have relied on oral family history, pictures, and personal recollections of my cousins and myself with respect to the Wagner family—their immigrant ancestors, the goals of our grandfather, the personalities of our grandparents, sibling achievements, and gender roles in the household. Heredity, birth order, education, and familial tradition can be powerful forces influencing the choices one makes, whether those choices are consciously and intentionally made or seemingly automatic and without forethought.

In addition to the impact of family, I have also paid attention to the urban context that would have influenced Aunt Dot. When she was born, Davenport was a small city. Though not cosmopolitan like New York or even Chicago, Davenport residents could not escape the news, activities, and behaviors going on in the world outside its borders. In an era without the ubiquity of social media that we know today, Aunt Dot, like other young women, would have absorbed social rules and norms from the church, newspapers, radio, and movies.

To help me reconstruct Aunt Dot's later adult life, I found and hired a professional researcher, Kimberly Tucker, who lives in Tampa and specializes in local resources. Over months of time, I asked questions. Usually, an answer to one question led to three further questions. The process became a lengthy and intense detective search, both for sources and for facts. Kimberly made suggestions, sometimes challenged my directions, and illumined interpretations. We became a team of collaborators. Eventually, we found more answers than dead ends and uncovered much of the context as well as the details to recreate the last half of my aunt's life.

However, uncovering facts about a woman's choices and behavior does not necessarily tell the motive and emotions behind a particular action or pattern of behavior. Because Aunt Dot left virtually no writing or thought in her own words, I have had to rely on inference from her family background, accepted attitudes and mores of middle-class women in her era, knowledge of expected behavior by the Lutheran church, and contemporary urban context. Where all sources were exhausted and no answers found, I have posed questions or suggested possible scenarios to create plausible interpretations for behavior that is factually unknown. In this role, I became the storyteller-turned-detective. This story is, then, to some degree a psychological analysis. In this realm I have been helped by insight gained over years of conversation with the Rev. Dr. Gary Wilkerson.

My collaboration with Gary began when I was trying to regain my balance after my husband's death. As an ordained Lutheran minister and former director of Mt. Olivet Lutheran Church Counseling Center in Minneapolis, Gary helped me to understand the significance of family dynamics and the effect of grief and loss on one's equilibrium. In the Epilogue he brings perspective to the strength and resilience shown by Aunt Dot, who demonstrated that she was a survivor.

Notes

- After verifying through the registrar's office at Carthage College that Aunt Dot had left at the end of two years and that August Gruhn had also been a student at the college during one of the years Aunt Dot attended, I began my search for her lost story with public documents pertaining to this first husband. Without a career history of her own that I knew about, I had to start tracing her through this husband.
- I thought that the national archive of the Evangelical Lutheran Church in America (ELCA) would be a logical and accessible starting point since August Gruhn had been a Lutheran minister. However, there had been several mergers of Lutheran churches during the twentieth century. I knew that Carthage College, then

in Illinois, had operated under the auspices of the former United Lutheran Church in America (ULCA), a body with long-established German ethnic roots. But the ULCA had been absorbed into the current ELCA as a result of two mergers decades earlier. I hoped that a national Lutheran archive had kept records of all of their ordained clergy, even though up to eight decades old. They had. Aunt Dot's story begins with some of the records about her first husband that are preserved in the ELCA archive.

- The denomination known as Lutheran referred to congregations and synods that had, typically, been organized around ethnic ties and geographical roots. Despite the end of open, mass immigration in the 1920s, the Lutheran church in this country grew amazingly. The following figures give some idea of its institutional power in the first third of the twentieth century. In his 2015 book, *Lutherans in America*, historian Mark Granquist states that the number of baptized Lutherans grew from 3.68 million in 1920 to 4.7 million fifteen years later. Also in 1935, there were 20,000 Lutheran congregations in America and 10,300 active Lutheran pastors. To prepare these pastors, there were twenty-six colleges and twenty-two theological seminaries. Having graduated from Carthage College, August Gruhn was attending one of these seminaries in 1935 (*Lutherans in America*, Minneapolis: Fortress Press, p. 235).

- The ULCA constituted the largest of the several bodies calling themselves Lutheran. During the period between the two world wars, it counted about 1.58 million members.

- The National Lutheran Council (NLC), organized in 1918, was a cooperative organization consisting of the ULCA and several other midwestern synods. Men wanting to enter the chaplaincy corps had to be approved by the NLC.

CHAPTER ONE

Betrayed

I was too young ever to meet August Gruhn, Aunt Dot's first husband. But I distinctly remember a service flag which hung in the large front room window of my grandparents' home on Brady Street in Davenport. Such flags hung in most living room windows during World War II. The flag consisted of a silky material with fringe on the bottom. A red border framed a white background on which the stars told passers-by the number of people from that home who were serving in the armed forces. Blue stars indicated that the men were fighting. Gold stars told the public that a member of the family had made the ultimate sacrifice and died for our country. The flag hanging in my grandparents' window had two blue stars—one for their son and one for their son-in-law.

World War II engaged the entire country—even school children. My other vivid memory is of taking coins to grade school in Rock Island to buy war stamps. One day every week was designated for the purchase. When I got home from school, I diligently pasted the stamps in a book. When the book was filled, my dad took me downtown to the bank where I could turn in my book of war stamps and receive a war bond in return. When even school children are encouraged to buy stamps and bonds to aid the war effort, you can be sure that the entire United States was pulling together.

In fact, all America became immediately and passionately patriotic when Pearl Harbor was attacked on Sunday, December 7, 1941. President Roosevelt called it a "date which will live in infamy." Aunt Dot's older brother, Dr. Eugene Christian Wagner, went down to the recruiting office in Des Moines, Iowa, on December 8, and volunteered for the army medical corps. Aunt Dot's husband, the Rev. August W. Gruhn, was serving his fifth year as an associate pastor of St. John's Lutheran Church in Des Moines, a very large church belonging to the Iowa Synod of the ULCA. Gruhn resigned that position in late January 1942 and applied for induction into the United States Army chaplaincy corps.

Our country had been at peace since the end of World War I in 1918. But ever since the unprovoked attack by the Empire of Japan, American men had been lining up by the thousands at recruiting centers across the country. There had been Lutheran ministers serving as chaplains in the armed forces since, at least, World War I. Now, it was clear that greater numbers of chaplains than ever before were going to be needed to serve our fighting men both spiritually and psychologically.

However, the process of becoming accepted into the chaplaincy corps was not determined simply by a man's individual desire and patriotic fervor. In the case of Rev. Gruhn, he had to verify that he was a naturalized citizen, since he had been born in Canada in 1910. Like all the men entering the army, he had to pass a physical exam. Next, he had to secure recommendations from his home church and synod. These requirements were not difficult for him to pass; they were merely time consuming. In fact, the letters, which had to be reviewed by members of the NLC in New York, were uniformly outstanding. One minister in Des Moines wrote: "Rev. Mr. Gruhn has many things to recommend him. In the first place he has a very pleasing personality and I am sure would win the confidence of the men." A member of the Iowa Synod from Nevada, Iowa, wrote: "Rev. Gruhn has a commanding personality and is a man of Christian character and integrity." In fact, all the letters of recommendation referred to the public persona of Rev. Gruhn as an individual of sterling character and extraordinary talent as a clergyman. Of course, all the letters of recommendation came from men in the church as well as in the world of business and commerce.

On March 5, 1942, Dr. Ralph Long, executive director of the NLC, wrote to the Area Chaplain of the Seventh Corps Army Headquarters in Omaha, Nebraska, saying that the council approved and endorsed the application of the Rev. August Wilfred Gruhn for appointment as a chaplain in the United States Army. Once the ecclesiastical endorsement came in, it was a foregone conclusion that the army would accept him into the chaplaincy corps.

Chaplain Gruhn served with distinction for the next five years, during which time he was promoted from Lieutenant to Captain to Major to Lieutenant Colonel. In fact, he was so successful that he was given executive responsibilities. One year he became an instructor in San Antonio, Texas, in a special course designed for prospective Air Force chaplains. Later, he became a supervising chaplain in the China–Burma–India Theater from July 1945 to June 1946, followed by a similar supervisory responsibility for several months in Europe. When the war ended in August 1945, the fighting men began coming home. The number of active duty chaplains was, similarly, reduced. Chaplain Gruhn was discharged in September 1947.

When going through Gruhn's file from the ELCA archive, I could find no mention of him going back into the parish ministry once he had been discharged from the army. That seemed odd to me, given his outstanding credentials. However, I did find the following letters written by him to church officials in 1950, when he was attempting to get back into the chaplaincy. I was not prepared for the contents of these letters.

Gruhn wrote to the Rev. Fred Boldt, President of the Iowa Synod of the ULCA, on October 11, 1950. In the letter, Gruhn explained first that he had been trying to return to the chaplaincy for the previous two years, but there had been no vacancies in his grade of Lieutenant Colonel. Now he finally had an upcoming interview. Because the church and army still required aspiring chaplains to have approval from the clergy, Gruhn explained to Boldt why he had been absent from synod meetings and had not previously been in communication with the synod president. It is clear that Gruhn's motivation in writing was to secure a favorable recommendation from Boldt for a return to the chaplaincy:

> During the past two years there has been an immense burden on me, and it is for this that I said I felt I should limit myself for now to military ministrations.
>
> After I had served as Supervising Chaplain with the Air Forces for a year-and-a-half in India–China–Burma and then in Europe, North Africa, and the Middle-East, I returned by air in October 1947 [sic] to attend for ten days the Chaplain Conference in Washington on temporary duty. It was at this time I found a completely intolerable situation in regard to my wife, totally incompatible with any proper concept of conduct for a ministerial family. In, brief, my home had been lost. You can well imagine that subsequently I felt lost too. This was a trying period through which I knew I must go. I wanted nothing more than to bury myself in solitude, and from the standpoint of the protection of the good name of my church and the Chaplaincy as well, to withdraw quietly away. I did not then and I do not now feel any urge at recrimination towards my wife. . . . From the standpoint of

Synod, the situation was only complicated by the fact that the family of Mrs. Gruhn were faithful members of Synod at Davenport and anything that might be said would only hurt and miserable [sic] grieve them in their old age. Therefore I make no further statement than to say that my future actions were scripturally founded, though I did my best to protect all concerned, and Mrs. Gruhn became soon after Mrs. R. Zambon of Tampa, Florida.

Also in October of 1950, as a part of his application for a return to the chaplaincy, Gruhn included the following undated letter to the Army-Navy Chaplain Commission of the ULCA and the NLC. In it Gruhn gave a more detailed explanation of the previous two years. His salutation was "Dear Brethren," and he gave the correct date of the Chaplain Conference as October 1946. His explanation began:

> . . . Upon calling my wife from Washington, I was immediately aware of a strained situation when she had resisted coming to Washington to meet me. I then went to Tampa, where she resided during my absence of more than a year and found a completely altered condition in my home, wholly incompatible with any true concept of the ministerial family, or any other. Much as I regret even at this time stating it, there had been an unaccountable, moral break-down, complicated by the fact that my wife, by her own admission, had undergone an abortion in a Tampa hospital, under an assumed name. All this, among other acts revealed at this time, provided a situation which I did not of course care to carry forward into the civilian ministry, and yet I sought means to conclude this matter with the least possible injury to all concerned, including my Church and the Chaplaincy. I decided to withdraw myself therefore for a time from all my former associations and, with the exception of my immediate family and of my very good friends, Chaplain (Major General) Charles I. Carpenter, Chief of Air chaplains, and Chaplain (Col. Ret.) Gynther Storaasli, former Chief of Air Chaplains, I was almost completely "incommunicado."
>
> I gave my wife one year to straighten her affairs, from October 1946 to September 1947, when my assignment to the European Headquarters ceased, though I told her that I could not return, again to make my home with her.

Having read Gruhn's allegations about Aunt Dot, I was initially confused. Given what I knew about her upbringing, the stern moral code in the Wagner household and in the Lutheran church, I couldn't believe that she had engaged in the behavior which Gruhn alleged. On the other hand, I knew that the war had resulted in fractured relationships in many families. Later, when I re-read Gruhn's letters and considered his sanctimonious-sounding tone, I became furious. He had attacked my aunt's character, and she couldn't have known about it. Moreover, these letters were held in a national church archive, available for the public to read. I became determined to find the truth about Aunt Dot's marriage, and I wondered who had betrayed whom.

To gain insight into Aunt Dot's character, I decided to review all that I had learned about the household, family, church, and local culture in which she had grown up. How did her father treat her as the only girl with three older brothers? What was the influence of her mother who had only finished seven grades of school before hiring out as a domestic? What other female role models did she have in her immediate family? What effect did it have on Aunt Dot to be growing up in the shadow of three smart, high-achieving older brothers? What effect did it have on her to come of age when women had the right to vote and were increasingly earning money by working outside the home in jobs other than that of being a domestic?

We cannot escape the influence of family and home. When growing up in an urban atmosphere, as opposed to village or farm, neither can we escape the impact of schools, neighborhoods, businesses, and media. To catch a glimpse of the Wagner family and the urban setting that was Davenport in the first third of the twentieth century, we turn to the next chapter.

Notes

- To gain a detailed and accurate picture of life in Davenport for the years in which Aunt Dot lived there, I am indebted to the Davenport Public Library, specifically it's Richardson-Sloan Special Collections Department. Their staff and resources provided all of the information I asked for with respect to populations, city directories, businesses, houses, schools, transportation, city maps, etc.
- For answers to innumerable questions about the Lutheran church over the past century, I am grateful to Joel Thoreson, archivist at

the ELCA national archive in Elk Grove Village, Illinois. He sent me all of the information on file for August Gruhn and promptly answered many questions about other chaplains as well as queries about particular congregations.

Aunt Dot's paternal grandmother, Louisa Stiel Wagner.

Aunt Dot's Family of Origin

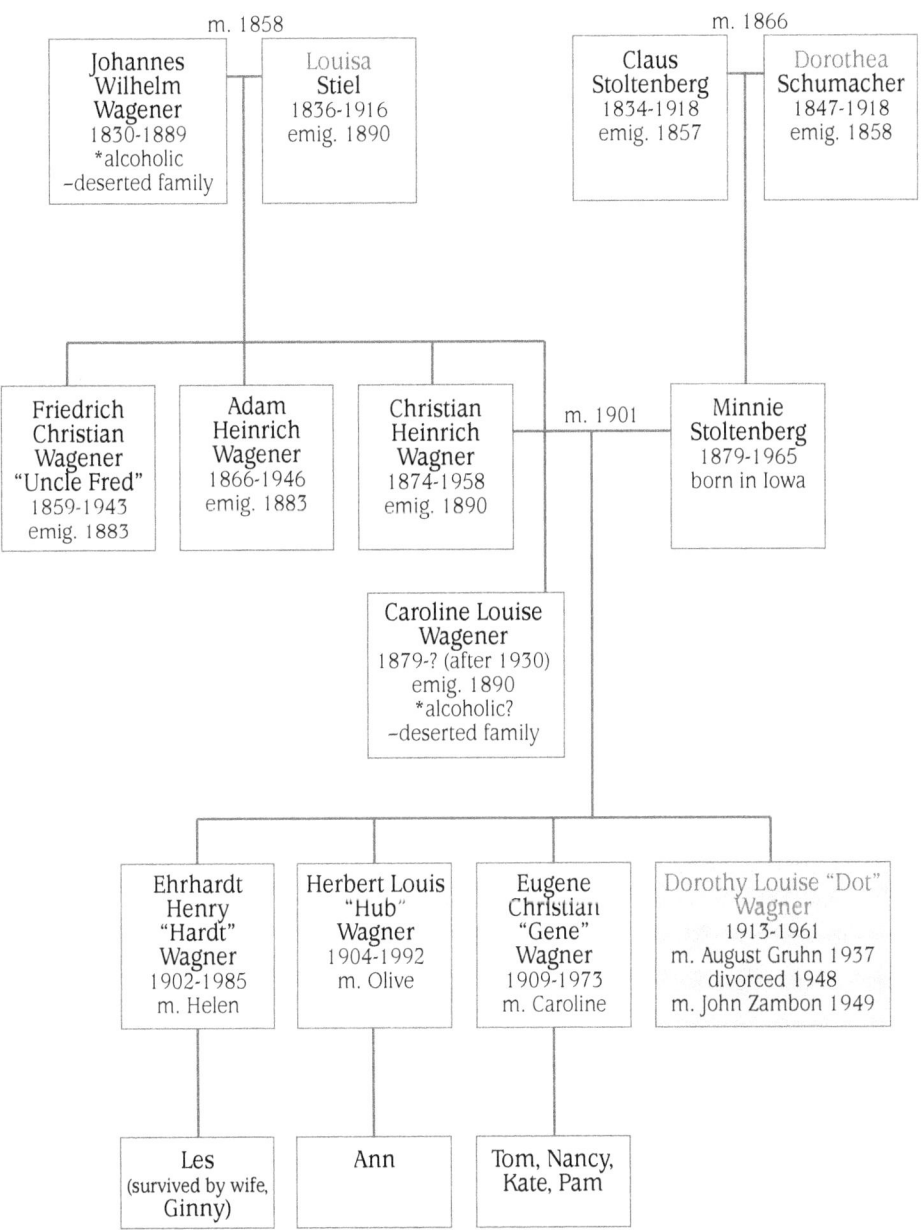

Growing Up German, Lutheran, and Female | 19

Aunt Dot is a child of about 5 years old in this picture, probably taken in 1918 on Uncle Fred's farm north of Davenport. Standing (left to right) are her cousins, Uncle Fred's grown daughters; her Aunt Kate in hat; and her mother, Grandma Wagner, on the far right. Seated (left to right) are Uncle Fred; Aunt Kate's husband, Uncle Jack; and Grandpa Wagner. On these visits to the farm, Aunt Dot would have been the only child among the family gathered for work and socializing.

Close scrutiny indicates that Aunt Kate is sporting a mustache to go along with the man's hat she is wearing. She probably inherited her mother's sense of humor. That would have been Aunt Dot's maternal grandmother, Dorothea Schumacher Stoltenberg.

CHAPTER TWO

Growing Up German, Lutheran, and Female

My grandparents named their last child and only daughter Dorothy Louise, after her two grandmothers. We cousins knew her simply as Aunt Dot. That name change followed a family pattern. Her oldest brother was named Ehrhardt Henry but was always called Hardt. The next oldest brother was my father. He was christened Herbert Louis but answered to the name of Hub. The third brother received the name Eugene Christian and was labeled Gene. Following that pattern of one syllable names, Dorothy Louise became Dot.

All of these Wagner siblings have their births recorded in the Scott County, Iowa, Register of Births, identified as Book 6 and dated January, 1897—December, 1917. Held in the office of the Clerk of Court, one might think that such a formal document provided accurate information, but that assumption would be a mistake. Dorothy Louise Wagner is recorded as "Wagner, Dorothy Louis" with an "M" written after the name to indicate gender male! Since the mother's name is correctly recorded as "Stoltenberg, Minnie" and the father as "Wagner, Christian," I knew for sure that the newborn was my Aunt Dot. But the gender error served as a lesson to make sure that I always had at least one other piece of accurate information to verify that what these old documents said was, in fact, true.

Born on February 6, 1913, Aunt Dot entered a household in which Hardt and Hub were well established in grade school. Hardt was ten-and-one-half years older; Hub eight-and-one-half years older. They had already been indoctrinated by their father. In his adult years, Hub recalled more than once that Grandpa would look at their report cards and say, "Well that is very good, but you can do better." We cannot say in what grades the boys were when this indoctrination began. Both boys were skipped ahead a year at some point. Davenport schools had been practicing this kind of promotion for several decades. In the case of Aunt Dot's two oldest brothers, they each graduated from high school at the age of sixteen. Though almost five years younger than Hub, Gene must have received the same kind of push from Grandpa, for he also graduated early from Davenport High School after being skipped ahead in the elementary grades. Aunt Dot was born into a family of smart brothers who were high achievers.

She was also born into a family who were staunchly Lutheran as well as German. Davenport's large number of German immigrants helped insure a Lutheran presence. Almost 400 years earlier, the German priest and university professor, Martin Luther, had preached and written about what he perceived to be evils in the Catholic church at that time. Thanks to the advent of the printing press, Luther's views spread like wildfire around Europe and precipitated the Protestant Reformation. Grandpa Wagner was baptized in Germany in the Lutheran church, known as the Evangelical Confessing Church. His school certificate, signed by both the teacher and the pastor, says that he was very regular in his church attendance in addition to getting very good marks.

Consistent with this early training, Grandpa made sure that his family in Davenport were all baptized and confirmed in St. Paul English Evangelical Lutheran Church, where the popular minister, Rev. W. H. Blancke, preached strong Lutheran morality in the English language. In the early twentieth century, many ethnic Lutheran churches struggled with the use of language. Should it be the native language from Europe or American English? It was a fierce struggle in many congregations, at least throughout the Midwest. Some immigrants were absolutely sure that God only paid attention to their prayers when they were uttered, for example, in the native Deutsch or Danish. But Grandpa had been drawn to St. Paul, in part, because Rev. Blancke was himself a German immigrant and also a college graduate. Probably even more to the point for Grandpa was the reality that Rev. Blancke preached to packed houses on the Chatauqua circuit about the evils of drink. Grandpa remembered that his father had been a "drunkard" in Germany and had deserted the family. When Grandpa was only five, he had been sent to live with an aunt in a nearby village, because his mother could not take care of him along with a newborn baby with no man around to earn a living. Powerful memories for a five-year-old boy!

Grandpa was also molded by the fact that he became a world traveler at a young age. In the spring of 1890, when he was 15½, Grandpa had finished the traditional schooling in Germany. He then traveled steerage from Bremerhavn, Germany, to Baltimore, Maryland, all by himself. Moreover, he had had to get to Bremerhavn by train, on his own, in order to catch the ship, Weser 2, that would take him to America. Even though his older brother, Fred, sent him money and directions, Grandpa still had to negotiate his passage alone. Then, when he had arrived in Baltimore, he had to get his tickets and train connections to Davenport—again by himself. And he spoke only German. Although probably people fluent in German were at the Baltimore terminal, ready to assist the young boy, being all alone in an unfamiliar and very large urban environment would have been scary. Having gotten the correct train west to Iowa, he would have had to transfer trains, at least in Chicago, perhaps at another place as well. Once in Davenport, he still had to catch one more train to travel the thirty miles north to Bennett, Iowa, where Fred was farming. Grandpa would have been very grateful to his older brother for saving him from having to do conscripted service in the Kaiser's army.

Grandpa farmed with his brother for a few years, but he did not have the big, rugged physique that characterized his older sibling. Probably also, he simply did not like farming. Grandpa's talent lay with numbers and business. Grandpa's drive to push ahead was evidenced by the fact that he moved into Davenport as soon as he could speak English and had met the residence and age requirements to file a Declaration of Intention to become a citizen. That meant he had to be at least 18 years of age. Not all immigrants became citizens. According to the Special Collections staff at the Davenport Library, well into the twentieth century fully 25 percent of immigrants had not yet become naturalized. But Fred Wagner had filed his papers and become a citizen exactly five years after entering the country. That was the legal minimum time for such action. Undoubtedly, he urged his younger brother to do the same.

Grandpa's citizenship document says that Christian Wagner appeared in District Court, meeting in Davenport on October 14, 1898. He proved to the court that he had come to the United States before he was 18 years old and that it had been his intention to become a citizen and "to renounce forever all allegiance to any foreign Prince, Potentate, State, or Sovereignty whatsoever, and particularly to **THE EMPEROR OF GERMANY**." Further, the court was satisfied that during the time he had resided in this country, he had "behaved as a man of good moral character, attached to the principles of the Constitution of the United States, and well disposed to the good order and happiness of the same. . . ."

By 1898, the first time his name appears in the *Davenport City Directory*, Grandpa had not only become a citizen, but he also had completed the course of study at Duncan's Business College and secured a job. According to the *City Directory*, he worked as a bookkeeper for the Davenport Ice Company, the office of which was located in the northwest part of the city where the German immigrants settled.

In addition to having a job, Grandpa also wanted a family. Probably recalling a broken home in his youth, he must have yearned for his own wife and children. As good fortune would have it, Grandpa met Minnie Stoltenberg in the neighborhood in which he worked and lived. Her family home was located across the street from Albrecht's Meat Market, which was next door to the office of the Davenport Ice Company. Since Davenport was then a city of neighborhoods, it is clear that Grandpa and Grandma met in the meat market or perhaps on the street or maybe down the block at the Washington Garden Beer Hall. They married in September 1901.

Actually, Grandpa had wanted to go back to Germany in 1900 to visit relatives and attend the World's Fair that was being held in Paris. He wanted to get married and take Grandma back with him. But she would have none of that. All her life, Grandma did not like to travel. Nonetheless, she agreed to wait while Grandpa made his trip. While waiting, she continued working, earning a livelihood by sewing. I found Grandma in the *City Directory* since women working on their own were typically listed there. Usually they were unmarried women or widows.

Once married, my grandparents moved immediately into the first house they owned, at 1408 Franklin Street, right in the middle of that German immigrant section of the city. Usually it was called Northwest Davenport, but sometimes colloquially was referred to as "Sauerkraut Hill." Grandma was still within two blocks of her Stoltenberg family home and Albrecht's Meat Market. Although Grandma liked the close family and neighborhood connection she had known all her life, the world around her was rapidly changing.

Located on the banks of the Mississippi River across from Rock Island, Illinois, where the river runs east and west, Davenport, Iowa, had become a small city by the time Aunt Dot was born. By 1910, the population had reached just over 43,000 residents. Amenities like telephones, electric lights, streetcars, and indoor plumbing had been in place for decades. Department stores like Harned and Von Maur, as well as J.H.C. Petersen, loomed large on the downtown streets. Daily newspapers, including one German-language paper, had been published for decades. German had been taught in the public schools since the 1860s. The German system of gymnastics, product of the Turner movement, had prevailed in the schools and community. Davenport residents were proud of their new high school, which had opened to a city-wide celebration in 1907, amid boasts of all the latest in facilities. Train travel had been prevalent for decades, always improving with speed and comfort. Thanks to a bridge over the Mississippi in the 1850s, Davenport had long served travelers going in all directions with train and inter-urban travel. Thus, it was hardly surprising that Theodore Roosevelt, the original Progressive, chose to stop and campaign in Davenport in 1912 when he ran as the third party presidential candidate on the Bull Moose ticket. Grandpa took 8-year old Hub, travelling by streetcar and foot, to Central Park to hear TR speak. Grandma, of course, stayed home with 3-year-old Gene; she may also have been pregnant with Aunt Dot. In any event, Grandma would not have been interested in politics.

Probably unusual for the era, when the adult lifespan was considerably shorter than it is today, Aunt Dot would have had dim childhood memories—fragments—of three grandparents. She would also have been told stories about these strong women. Grandpa Wagner's mother, Louisa Stiel Wagner, lived with her oldest son, Fred Wagner, and his family on their farm north of Davenport. She had been a survivor, having borne ten children but seeing six of them die before adulthood. All this while she also coped with an alcoholic husband and, probably, abuse over the years. Thanks to the surrogate father role that her oldest son assumed, Louisa was able to emigrate to America with her 11-year-old daughter, Caroline Louise, in 1890. They settled with Fred and his growing family in Cedar County Iowa.

By all accounts, Fred Wagner exemplified traditional German traits of energy, discipline, and hard work. Certainly these characteristics were accentuated by being a penniless immigrant and the son of an alcoholic father. Assuming the role of parent to his siblings and devoted son to his mother, Fred labored diligently to pay off emigration costs and then buy his own farm. He accomplished all this between 1890 and 1903. Grandpa, undoubtedly, looked up to this older brother as a model of industry and ambition.

Each summer in the new century, when his boys were old enough to travel, Grandpa would take his family by train north to Bennett, Iowa, where the farm was located. The thirty-mile train trip, with intermediate stops along the way, was long enough that Grandma always packed a lunch. The three brothers thought this was a big adventure. Once on the farm, there were two boy cousins to play with, in addition to learning about the animals and helping out with farm work. Aunt Dot would have had one or two recollections of her grandmother as a small, frail-looking old lady who died at the age of 80 in 1916. She certainly would have heard stories about her grandmother from her older girl cousins on the farm, because Louisa had lived and worked with them for almost twenty years.

Aunt Dot would definitely have remembered her maternal grandparents, who lived only three blocks from the Wagner home and just across from Albrecht's Meat Market. Claus and Dora Stoltenberg had seven grandsons nearby but only one young granddaughter before Aunt Dot was born. However, that 4-year-old girl lived several blocks away from the grandparents. Their oldest granddaughter lived next door, but she was already in her teen years. Chances are, Claus and Dora would have been overjoyed that their daughter, Minnie, had finally given birth to a daughter and lived so close by.

Claus had been born in the province of Holstein, near Kiel, Germany, in September 1834. He came to America on the Copernicus, a three-masted sailing ship called a "barque." Traveling steerage class, the lowest form of human existence on an immigrant ship, Claus departed from Hamburg, Germany, on September 2, 1857. The ship docked in New Orleans on November 7, 1857. He then caught a riverboat north, up the Mississippi to Davenport, arriving on November 20. He worked as a laborer until volunteering for the Union Army in August 1861. Entering as a private, he was twice promoted, to be mustered out with the rank of sergeant after a three-year term of service. When he came home to Davenport, Claus Stoltenberg met and married Dora Schumacher on September 22, 1866. He was 32, she 19 years of age.

Claus worked as a laborer, including serving as a foreman for the city grain elevator, until ill health forced him to cut back. Like so many Union Army soldiers who had served in Arkansas, Claus contracted malaria, then called "intermittent fever." It affected him the remainder of his life. He probably also contracted rheumatic fever; medical reports in his pension file indicate that he suffered, sometimes for weeks in winter months, of what was diagnosed as rheumatism, a general term then used to cover a number of inflammation maladies. Gradually, Claus' health declined so that by the turn of the century he was not able to support his wife and children on the pay of a laborer, since he could only do "one quarter" of a man's work. He received an "invalid pension" from the federal government but managed to serve for years as janitor of the city hall. It was light duty compared to his previous physical labor. In this role, Claus was well-liked and well-known among city officials. When he died on Sunday morning, February 17, 1918, the eight-column-inch obituary in the Monday evening edition of *The Davenport Democrat and Leader* carried the headline, "LAST TAPS FOR CIVIL WAR VET." Aunt Dot would have just turned 5 years of age when her grandfather died.

Like her husband, Dora (whose full name was Dorothea Schumacher Stoltenberg) had come to America on a sailing ship, also surviving in steerage class. However, she travelled with her widowed father and three older siblings. Dorothea was only 11 years old when the family left Germany in April 1858. She had been born on July 12, 1847, in East Holstein, almost on the Baltic coast, to a family who were farmers. Her mother had died when the child was only 8. Her older sister, Anna, served as a surrogate mother on the trip and in this country until the young girl got married.

In addition to nursing Claus through his periodic bouts of ill health, grieving the death of two children, managing to feed and clothe six surviving children, and keeping house for years with no running water and no electricity, Dora managed to retain a sense of humor. She and the neighborhood women would congregate periodically at Albrecht's Meat Market and weigh themselves on the big scale there. When it was Dora's turn to step on the scale, she always managed to hold two irons under her apron so that she weighed a lot more than she actually did. When Grandma Wagner told me this story, she chuckled at the recollection. No doubt over the years, Grandma told Aunt Dot this and many other stories about Dora and Claus.

At some point in her young life, Aunt Dot also learned about a medal Grandma had received when she was in seventh grade. Saved by Aunt Dot, and subsequently saved by members of the Zambon family in Florida, the medal was awarded to Wilhelmina Stoltenberg in 1891 for "attendance" and "deportment." Information from the Davenport School Museum reports that it was a Kuhnen Medal, named for Nicholas Kuhnen, a wealthy German immigrant. He had emigrated to Davenport in the 1850s and become a very successful cigar manufacturer. Kuhnen also served for several years on the Davenport school board and thought that children should be encouraged to become good citizens. To that end, he donated $1,000 in the late 1880s to create an endowed fund.

From the proceeds, medals were to be struck and awarded annually to one student in each of the city's schools. Medal recipients were selected by the principal and/or teachers of each school. The students selected were always in the last year of school (some schools in Davenport included eight grades, but some only seven). Grandma's medal says 7th Grade. According to the Director of the Davenport School Museum, each medal consisted of one ounce of pure silver. Grandma's medal was fashioned as a pin that could be worn on a lapel.

Having completed seven grades, Grandma Wagner, out of tradition and necessity, had quit school and begun work as a domestic in big homes in Davenport. That pattern was common in the later 1800s for women from a working-class background. Perhaps being selected to receive the Kuhnen Medal even served as a kind of recommendation for Grandma; the medal certainly stood for responsibility and reliability. With Claus ill periodically, Grandma, like her older sister Kate, had to go to work and help contribute to the family income. Grandma had been born in March 1879 and named Wilhelmina, but she was always known as Minnie. However, the *Davenport City Directory* for 1894-95 gives two listings, one as "Miss Minnie Stoltenberg" and one as "Miss Wilhelmina Stoltenberg." In both instances, she is listed as a "domestic" but living at the small family home on Leonard Street in northwest Davenport.

A few years later, the final *City Directory* for the century records Grandma as working for the R. Kraus Company, but still living at the family home. This company was a manufacturer and wholesaler of cloth and tailor's trimmings. They made a variety of men's work clothes and upholstery furnishings. A couple of years later, when Grandma knew that she would be married, the directory lists her as "seamstress," working on her own, out of the family home. Thus Grandma, though short on formal education, had several years of practical schooling in household arts and money management before she got married.

The home and family into which Aunt Dot was born reflected traditional gender roles as people knew them at that time. Men left the home each morning and went to their jobs in the world of business and commerce. Grandpa had been trained as a bookkeeper, but exhibited an entrepreneurial spirit. Early in the new century, he ventured into the china and housewares business as an employee of the Western China Co. in Davenport. Within a few years, he and others organized their own company known as Department A. They leased the fifth floor of Harned and Von Maur and sold, according to their letterhead stationary, "dinnerware, house furnishings, glassware, cameras, photographic supplies, sporting goods, toys and dolls."

While Grandpa was working in downtown Davenport, Grandma was busy running her household. In a world with few labor-saving devices, she devoted each day to a different activity. This strategy undoubtedly proved an efficient, as well as necessary, economy of time and labor. For example, Monday was wash day. Tuesday naturally became the day for ironing. Wednesday was probably reserved for sewing and mending, Thursday for cleaning the entire house, and Friday for baking. Saturday could be the day for catching up. Sunday, of course, meant a day of rest, reserved for church and family. In addition to this weekly plan of organization, Grandma had to visit the meat market several times a week, since freezers were an unheard-of invention in the 1910s. Food was kept cool in an icebox. Women had to signal the iceman when they needed a new block of ice by hanging a sign in the window. Milk also was delivered to the house by a horse-drawn wagon. All these necessities fell to Grandma, who had to prepare three meals daily for growing and presumably always hungry boys.

Since she had had to work as a domestic from the time she was 12 or 13, it seems clear that Grandma would have expected Aunt Dot to help run the household from the time she was able to satisfactorily perform simple tasks. For example, a child of eight could have learned to make beds, carry dirty clothes down to the basement for washing, and dust furniture. Aunt Dot would also have learned how to prepare simple foods, set the table, and help wash and wipe dishes. It also seems clear that Grandma would not have asked her sons to help with women's work, though they could have been asked to carry heavy loads of wet clothes out to the backyard to be hung on the line by Grandma.

Following traditional gender roles, the cooking fell to Grandma with only two exceptions that we cousins know about. If the supper was to be potato pancakes, Grandpa would peel a peck of potatoes for the meal. On the rare occasion that Grandma was not home for supper, Grandpa would go to the meat market and buy a steak which he would fry in butter, much to the delight of his growing sons. When Grandma came home, the young boys would tell her how wonderful the steak tasted. Grandma's response was to harrumph and mutter, "Anyone can cook with butter." However, Grandpa had his comeback. When, on the rare evening that Grandma's meal was not up to her usual excellent cooking, Grandpa's comment would be: "*Es lass sich essen.*" Literally translated, "It permits itself to be eaten." Such give and take between Grandma and Grandpa was not mean-spirited.

It translated to us cousins as two adults who each managed their own areas of the marriage very well and who respected their spouse.

Despite the apparently smooth-running Wagner household in northwest Davenport, world events soon intruded and dramatically affected both city and family. Although the year 1913 was, on the whole, peaceful in the United States, ancient rivalries had been simmering in Europe for several years. When the Austrian Archduke Francis Ferdinand and his wife were killed by Serbian assassins in June 1914, that event proved to be the match igniting a world war. By the end of October, the conflict that had begun between Serbia and Austria had escalated into a world conflict involving countries and powers on six continents.[1] The causes were complex in terms of European treaties and rivalries, but in the view of many Americans, Germany soon became the clear villain. The country divided into isolationists and interventionists, but when German U-boats sank the Lusitania, in May 1915, with 100 Americans on board, widespread anti-German hysteria broke out.

In Davenport and in Iowa, the hysteria kept growing. Local school officials cut out all German language classes after the 1916-17 school year. Some universities eliminated their German Departments. "...German books were withdrawn from public library circulation, and German publications driven under cover. The Governor of Iowa even promulgated an edict that 'conversation in public places, on trains, or over the telephone should be in the English language.'"[2] In the Wagner household, the boys were old enough to remember one night at the dinner table when Grandpa made a formal announcement that no more German would be spoken in the house. About five minutes later, when a water faucet was heard to be loudly dripping, Grandpa blurted out in German, "Who left that faucet on?" Of course, everyone laughed. In the extreme, some anti-German hysteria resulted in people re-naming sauerkraut "liberty cabbage."[3] As we know, America was inexorably drawn into the conflict. Congress declared war on the German Empire in the wee hours of the morning on April 6, 1917. Ironically, that day was Good Friday.

Concurrent with this anti-German hysteria was the reality that Grandpa experienced a major loss in his business. He had invested, with others, in the company called Department A. Probably due to a partner-

---

[1] Carlton J.H. Hayes, *A Political and Cultural History of Modern Europe*, vol. 2 (New York: The Macmillan Company, 1937), 782.
[2] Samuel Eliot Morison and Henry Steele Commager, *The Growth of the American Republic*, vol. 2 (New York: Oxford University Press, 1950), 477.
[3] Vincent J. Cannato, *American Passage: The History of Ellis Island* (n.p.: Harper, 2009), 308.

ship of Harned and VonMaur with the Petersen Company, Department A was squeezed. Though a manager, Grandpa did not have controlling interest. His partners bought him out. It must have been a devastating loss to Grandpa. His career had, seemingly, been on the rise since he had graduated from Duncan's Business College more than a decade earlier. To be squeezed out would have been a serious blow to his ego and loss of steady income for the family. We do not know what affected his decision, but he made up his mind to move to Cedar Rapids, about sixty miles west of Davenport. Perhaps he thought a totally new start would be best. Perhaps he thought that there would be less anti-German feeling in Cedar Rapids. Perhaps he was affected by the fact that Rev. Blancke had resigned from the pulpit of St. Paul and moved out of town.

Whatever the primary motivation, Grandpa sold their house in northwest Davenport and moved the family to Cedar Rapids for the school year beginning in 1917. Hardt would have been 15, Hub 13, Gene 8, and Aunt Dot 4½ that fall. She would have remembered that they moved, but not known exactly why until she got older. Grandma had never lived outside Davenport, so this would have been very threatening to her. Her father, Claus Stoltenberg, was not in good health. In Cedar Rapids, she was sixty miles away from him instead of three blocks distant. Everyone in the family was faced with something new. Grandpa decided on a new career, taking a butter-maker into partnership and opening a retail butter and egg store. Grandma had to furnish a new house and try to make it comfortable for everyone when she herself was not happy. The boys all had to begin new schools. As a 4 year old, Aunt Dot would have felt and internalized the emotions related to change, loss, fear, unhappiness, and insecurity.

As sometimes happens, when the head of the family makes such a radical decision, the situation does not always turn out well. From what we cousins learned in later years, Grandpa simply did not like the butter and egg business. There may have been more to it, but the decision was made to return to Davenport after a year. Grandpa went back to work as a bookkeeper. The family moved into the former Stoltenberg home on Leonard Street, when it became vacant, due to the death of both grandparents. Hardt entered high school in the fall of 1918 as a senior. Hub enrolled as a sophomore. Gene would have gone back to Jackson elementary school, which he had attended before the family moved. Aunt Dot would have started at the same school. She would have been 5½ in the fall of 1918. If starting school felt scary, Aunt Dot would have had Gene to walk to school with her. On November 11, when the war ended, no doubt the whole family, as well as all of Davenport and the entire nation, was relieved and celebrating. Everyone wanted stability and a return to normality.

In the spring after the Armistice was signed, Hardt graduated from Davenport High School at the age of 16. None of his cousins had finished high school; it was not necessary to do so at that time in order to get a job. But Hardt not only had graduated, he also had completed the Latin course, which was then considered the college preparatory course. Moreover, in a graduating class of 113, Hardt was one of only three men who earned "First Honors." In the fall he was destined to head south about 100 miles to enroll in Carthage College, then located in the small town of Carthage, Illinois.

We cousins never heard our grandfather or fathers talk about why they were sent to Carthage College when other schools were much nearer to home. Right across the Mississippi in Rock Island was a Lutheran institution known as Augustana College. It was well established and enjoyed a good reputation. Hardt could have lived at home and taken a streetcar across the river to attend classes. That would have saved the cost of board and room. A second choice that could have been explored was the University of Iowa, located in Iowa City, about sixty miles west of Davenport and close to Cedar Rapids where the family had resided for a year. As an Iowa resident, Hardt could have saved on the cost of tuition. It seems clear in hindsight, and in the absence of any oral history, that Grandpa had decided on Carthage College due to the influence of Rev. Blancke, the well-respected minister who had held the pulpit of St. Paul English Evangelical Lutheran Church for just over two decades. Moreover, he had married Grandpa and Grandma in 1901. Perhaps Grandpa looked on him as a kind of surrogate father.

W. H. Blancke had emigrated from Germany and attended Carthage College, graduating in the class of 1883. Subsequently, he had served as field secretary for the college, helping to attract students to the fledgling institution. By 1901, Blancke was serving on the board of trustees for the college. A year later, he became president of the board, a role he held for a decade. Thus, he was well positioned to urge and advise Grandpa regarding the importance of college in general and Carthage College in particular. It had been started by and continued with support from German Lutheran synods in the East and the Midwest. In contrast, Augustana College, though Lutheran in denominational affiliation, celebrated a Swedish background. The University of Iowa was a secular, state-supported institution. So, it seems that Rev. Blancke's persuasion, plus the German and Lutheran heritage, cast the dye for Hardt to go to Carthage College.

Given the expense of travelling to and attending a private church college, it is clear that total dollar cost was not the decisive factor in settling on Carthage College. Grandpa had gone through a business loss just two years earlier, followed by complete family upheaval when they moved to Cedar Rapids for only one year and then back to Davenport. Grandpa again went back to work as a bookkeeper with a monthly wage. However, he probably had some capital; his partners in Department A Company had bought him out in 1917. In addition, he had sold the house on Franklin Street when the family moved to Cedar Rapids. He must have set aside money for the boys' college education at some point, and that money must have remained untouched. One clue to Grandpa's determination comes from a comment by Hub in his adult years, "It was always understood we were going to college."

Grandpa's goal of sending his children to college seems a logical extension of his own inner drive to succeed, having experienced his own father's drunkenness and desertion of the family in Germany. Yet Grandpa's inner drive was reinforced by the urban times in which the family lived. His brother Fred's sons went into farming like their father. At that time, they didn't need a college degree. They just needed to be smart, hard-working, disciplined, and persevering like their father had been. Being a Davenport businessman with an entrepreneurial spirit and influenced by Rev. Blancke, Grandpa probably saw that a college education could unlock career doors, at least, for his sons. Especially when combined with his early indoctrination: ". . . you can do better."

Whether or not Hardt was excited or nervous about going off to college, we have no way of knowing. What the rest of the family thought about this adventure is also unknown. Grandma was unfamiliar with the whole idea of a college education. The men in her family had been tradesmen or laborers. She would, very likely, have concentrated her efforts toward getting Hardt's clothes ready for his trip and sending some food along with him. Hub would have known that in two years, his turn would come. So he may have been quite excited at Hardt's new, upcoming experience. Though only 10 years old, Gene certainly knew that his turn would eventually come. At age 6½, we can imagine that Aunt Dot did not fully understand the impact of what was happening in the household. But going away to college could have sounded exciting. Maybe she was told that her turn would come. At the very least, she certainly would have noticed Hardt's absence from the house on a daily basis.

Yet sending his sons to college was not Grandpa's only goal. Within two years of returning to Davenport in the fall of 1918, Grandpa also purchased a larger house and re-purchased Department A Company. By the time Hardt came home from his first year in college, in the spring of 1920, the family had moved into their new home at 2925 Brady Street, north and east of the German neighborhood of northwest Davenport. Instead of being just fifteen blocks north of the river, they were now twenty-nine blocks north—in fact several blocks north of Central Park where Teddy Roosevelt had spoken in 1912. By 1920 it had been renamed Vander Veer Park. When Grandpa managed to buy back Department A Company, he gained controlling interest. According to listings in the *City Directory*, he seems to have accomplished all this between the fall of 1918 and the same time two years later. He is listed as a bookkeeper in the 1919 *City Directory* but is cited as a department manager with Harned and Von Maur in 1920.

Probably because his sons were growing up, Grandpa decided to buy a larger house than the one in which they had lived in northwest Davenport. A square, two-story frame structure sat atop a terrace that necessitated climbing about ten steps to arrive in the front yard. The house featured a large front porch, a basement, and an attic. It provided more bedrooms for the boys but also more work for Grandma. The main floor consisted of a large living room with a bay window that overlooked the front lawn. Behind the front room, a generous dining room and spacious kitchen surely made Grandma happy when serving meals. Wide, open stairs started inside the front door and led to the second floor, which accommodated three bedrooms and one large bathroom. Enclosed stairs led from the front bedroom to an attic that allowed for two beds and dressers plus storage. Grandma had a backyard in which to hang her washing, but she also had to make many, many trips up and down stairs doing laundry and cleaning.

Probably Hub, Gene, and Aunt Dot enjoyed having more space; the new house must have seemed like a palace compared to the former, small Stoltenberg home where they had lived temporarily. Aunt Dot would have had her own bedroom on the second floor, with her parents in an adjoining bedroom. Perhaps when Hardt was off at college, Hub and Gene shared the remaining bedroom on the second floor. When he came home from college, someone had to sleep in the attic. But some summers, Hardt worked for his older cousin on the farm in Bennett. So sleeping in the attic would not have been a daily diet. With no insulation, the attic proved excessively hot in the summer.

Whether or not Gene and Aunt Dot enjoyed going to a new school, we have no way of knowing. Grant School was located just a few blocks west of their new home. Both siblings would have walked; school buses did not exist in the city. It was probably easier for Gene to adjust, as the older and more experienced brother. We simply do not know how shy Aunt Dot was and how easily she made new friends. We can be sure that she paid attention in classes and did everything the teacher said to do. She could not have been totally immune from Grandpa's dictum, "You can do better." In addition, she would also have had to pay attention to Grandma's instructions about housework in the new home. No doubt her household tasks increased in amount and complexity with her growing years, skill, and knowledge. But Aunt Dot's world at age 7 in 1920 had nothing in common with Hardt's world as a freshman in college.

Life at Carthage College would have seemed totally foreign to Hardt upon arriving in September 1919. The town of Carthage, county seat of Hancock County, was thriving, but the population totaled only about 1500 citizens. By contrast, Davenport had had a population of over 43,000 by 1910. In 1920, over 56,700 residents called the city home. Carthage would have seemed like a village. There were no streetcars, no large department stores, and no neighborhoods like northwest Davenport. Hardt could easily have walked from the train station to the college, perhaps a distance of one mile, carrying a single suitcase. The campus was small—a president's home, the ubiquitous Old Main that graced all early college campuses, a science building, a gymnasium building, and a dormitory each for men and women. The formal entrance to the campus was announced by two square, brick columns standing guard on the north side of what the locals called "the hard road," the main artery leading into and out of town. A circular drive around the interior of the campus permitted cars to pull up to each building. Stately evergreens flanked either side of the long walk, leading through the center of campus from the formal entrance to the Old Main building, the heart of the academic enterprise—housing library, classrooms, registrar's office, and business office. The science building, completed in 1912, had classrooms plus laboratories for chemistry, biology, and physics. The three-story women's dormitory had been finished in 1918 and featured accommodations for 130 female students, formal parlors for entertaining and receptions, as well as a dining room where all the students ate sit-down meals on white tablecloths. Students served as waiters for the tables and also as dishwashers and kitchen help.

A gymnasium had been erected in 1905 but was small by our standards today, though considered "one of the finest in the Middle West for a school of the type of Carthage."[4] Carthage College had produced inter-collegiate athletics teams for several years. Beyond these few buildings and dormitories, there was ample space for football, baseball, track, and tennis—so much space, in fact, that a vigorously kicked football could have been lost in the cornfields, which backed up the goalposts at one end of the field.

In addition to athletics, the college supported extra-curricular activities like literary societies, Christian associations, social fraternities and sororities, dramatic club, inter-collegiate debate, a student newspaper, and musical events including a touring choir. Trinity Lutheran Church, located near the town square, served as the college church for students from Lutheran homes. Additional local churches welcomed students from other denominations. Students were also expected to attend daily chapel on campus.[5]

With respect to its curriculum, Grandpa would have heard from Rev. Blancke that Carthage College had been accredited in 1916 and received an A+ rating by the examiners, who represented the North Central Association of Colleges and Secondary Schools and applied that accrediting organization's standards. Only four other colleges in Illinois had received an A+ rating:

> Under this rating, credits earned at Carthage could be transferred at full value to all universities and graduate schools in the country for undergraduate and graduate study.

Achieving such a rating required the college to have no less than eight academic departments, each headed by at least one full-time professor. The requirement to be a professor stated that the person had to have completed graduate study "equal to that required for a master's degree at the University of Illinois." In fact, Carthage had several faculty holding doctoral degrees, and usually the curriculum included nine or more departments.[6]

Though not personally familiar with college curricula, Grandpa would have understood that Carthage College, though small, was academically

---

[4] William Carl Spielman, *The Diamond Jubilee History of Carthage College 1870-1945* (Carthage, Illinois: College Historical Society, 1945), 91.

[5] Spielman, 110.

[6] Spielman, 98 and 108-9.

rigorous. Undoubtedly, this reality, combined with the German Lutheran heritage and on-going support of church synods, must have convinced him that he had made the best possible college choice for his sons. Hub travelled with Hardt to campus in the fall of 1921. Like Hardt, he was young for an entering freshman. He turned 17 on September 20, about three weeks after classes started.

Both Wagner brothers proved to be exceptional in academics as well as athletics. They both excelled particularly in football and basketball. They were each elected president of their respective classes during one of their college years. Perhaps most outstanding, they each received some grades of A+. Grade inflation, as we know it today, did not exist then. A grade of C was respectable and average. Yet Hardt received several grades of A+ on his mathematics courses. Showing differences in sibling talents and interests, Hub received his grades of A+ in languages. While total enrollment at Carthage College hovered between 300 and 350 students, it was less than at Davenport High School. Fewer students could have meant less competition for grades. But Carthage represented a well-accredited college, not high school curriculum and faculty.

Further substantiating the academic ability of the Wagner brothers is the fact that the faculty voted them to be recipients of the Carthage College Scholarship to the University of Illinois for graduate study. Hardt finished his master's degree in 1924, with a major in mathematics, and was advised to go on to the University of Michigan at Ann Arbor to pursue a Ph.D. Hub completed his master's degree in 1926 with a major in history. Clearly both Wagner brothers had taken to heart Grandpa's early admonition, "You can do better." They had each earned their first graduate degrees by age 22.

Aunt Dot turned 13 in February 1926. Her life in eighth grade was a world away from her two older brothers with their graduate degrees. By contrast, she had just completed her confirmation course at St. Paul Lutheran Church. Yet she would have known that Carthage College was a co-ed institution, and she would have understood that there were degrees beyond a college baccalaureate. At the same time she would also have known about and absorbed some of what had been happening in the country outside of academe.

Following the end of World War I, people became euphoric. Business boomed, and the whole populace reveled in a new release of inhibitions and a sense of optimism, as well as radically altered roles and images for women. To what degree Aunt Dot was affected by such changes at the time, we can merely surmise. She was only 7 years old in February 1920, but she was growing up in a milieu very different from the one in which Grandma had grown up. Moreover, the effect of the 1920s on Aunt Dot was also very different from the effect on her older brothers. They were still concerned with education, jobs, business, sports, and politics. The roles of boys and men had changed very little from previous decades. By contrast, Aunt Dot grew up learning that she no longer had to be relegated to house and home. Girls graduated from high school and went on to college. Some held jobs beyond the traditional roles of teacher, nurse, secretary, and saleslady.

This changing milieu began with congress and state legislatures. The first of two constitutional amendments that affected the entire country came into being on January 29, 1919, when the Eighteenth Amendment to the Constitution was ratified. Women, in particular, had been campaigning for decades to make the country dry. With passage of this Prohibition Amendment, people throughout the country felt that, at last, the citizenry would be better off. Time would prove that point of view overly optimistic. Of course, for the Wagner household, passage of prohibition made no change in behavior of family members. The household had always been dry and would remain that way. In fact, Grandpa had promised each of his sons a gold watch if they would refrain from alcohol and cigarettes before the age of 21. In 1919, for the country at large, the sale of alcohol simply went underground. The old-time saloon that catered to men only gave way to the speakeasy, where the correct password and known visage allowed entry. The newly liberated female entered with her male companion and enjoyed the new cocktails then popular in the decade.

The constitutional change that specifically intended to liberate women followed soon on the heels of prohibition. The Nineteenth Amendment, ratified on August 26, 1920, finally granted women the right to vote, after a struggle of some eighty years. That did not mean that women flocked to the polls in the presidential election of 1920, but they had right to do so. We cousins never heard whether or not Grandma ever voted. I suspect she may not have, but we don't know for sure. Aunt Dot, on the other hand, came of age knowing that she was a woman, with every right and responsibility to vote in all elections, just as her older brothers did.

Helping to publicize such national news was the new medium of radio. Early crystal sets, where one wore headphones, enabled the listener to hear the national election results in 1920. The Westinghouse Electric and Manufacturing Company in Pittsburgh broadcast the Harding-Cox presidential race on November 2. Widespread refining of broadcasting, as well as production of parts, and reduction in the cost of manufacturing, soon made this new voice of the country a common phenomenon. By the end of the decade, one estimate claimed that radio reached into every third home in the country.[7] In fact, the census of 1930 asked people if they had a radio in their home. The Wagners did, but it seems very likely that Aunt Dot grew up in a household that had possessed a radio from an early date. They may even have had one of the first crystal sets, because Davenport and Brady Street were in the forefront of broadcasting development.

The first licensed commercial radio station in the country came into being in 1920 when KDKA, owned by Westinghouse in Pittsburgh, went on the airwaves. Two years later, on February 18, 1922, Davenport became home to the second licensed commercial station in the country. Radio WOC broadcast from its location on the campus of the Palmer School of Chiropractic, on the Brady Street hill, about eighteen blocks south of the Wagner home at 29th and Brady. Then in 1924, WOC broadcast the first "chain program" nationally; 1300 miles of wire connected Davenport with station WEAF in New York City. Two years later, the National Broadcasting Company was formed; WOC became the local affiliate.[8]

As with any newfangled invention, people wondered if radio would last. Maybe it was just a fad, like many of the 1920s activities, e.g. flagpole sitting or marathon dancing. Some were sure that the novelty would eventually wear off of hearing a jazz orchestra in Schenectady or in Davenport play "Mr. Gallagher and Mr. Shean." The novelty did not wear off. To their weekly broadcast schedule of music, radio managers added hours of news, as well as sports events, talks, quiz shows, and "soap operas." Listeners around the country could feel the thrill in the moment when Babe Ruth hit yet another home run or Knute Rockne's Notre Dame football teams, with their famous "four horsemen," scored yet another victory. Since one of those "four horsemen" was a Davenport boy, we can be sure that Hub and Gene followed the Fighting Irish. At home, Aunt Dot and her parents could sit in their house and hear news from around the country. The women could also prepare food and mend or knit while enjoying music or absorbing events of the day. Listening to the radio was definitely not a waste of time.

---

[7] Paul Sann, *The Lawless Decade* (New York: Crown Publishers, Inc., 1957), 38-9.
[8] Marlys Svendsen, *Davenport: A Pictorial History 1836-1986* (n.p.: G. Bradley Publishing, Inc., 1985), 147.

For the nation as a whole, radio ended the relative isolation of people on farms, in small towns, or in sparsely populated areas of the country. News or sports events or sermons provided daily and weekly conversation topics when folks got together. Although newspapers or magazines could give the same information in print, the added dimension of sound in musical tone, or audience cheering at a game, or vocal expression in the voice of a talented broadcaster simply made the entire experience come alive in ways that the printed page could not accomplish. Dollar figures in radio sales, parts, and accessories tell the success story. Such annual sales for 1922 amounted to $60,000,000. By 1929, the same total sales had reached $842,548,000. That was an increase of 1400 percent.[9]

The success of radio sales in the decade of the twenties also tells the story of an economic boom that actually began in 1919, after the end of the war. Several factors aided this meteoric rise. A general sense of euphoria pervaded the country when the boys came marching home. President Harding pronounced that there would be a return to "normalcy." The advent of advertising and skilled salesmen persuaded the public that there were many new products which they should have. Magazines, as well as newspapers and soon radio, assisted the skilled salesman in pushing the public to buy. And the advent of buying on time proved too alluring to pass up.

In addition to radio, the other amazing invention of the decade was the merging of sound with movies. Moving pictures had been around for a couple of decades, but dialogue was silent. Lines spoken by the actors were printed on the screen. Usually, a pianist played music that tried to portray the emotion depicted on the screen. In 1927, when Hollywood technology found out how to synchronize sound with motion, a whole new genre developed, known as the movie musical. Actors and actresses gained fame and money based on their vocal expression as well as their looks plus acting and dancing talent.

We don't know whether or not the Wagner brothers went to the movies in that significant year, but 1927 proved pivotal for the brothers and Aunt Dot. In the spring of that year, Hub received a call from the President of Carthage College, asking him to join the faculty that fall as an instructor in history and assistant coach in three sports. He turned 23 years old that September; Gene had turned 18 in June of that year. Thus, the two brothers set out for Carthage College in the fall, one as a freshman student and the other as a freshman faculty member. That left Aunt

---

[9] Frederick Lewis Allen, *Only Yesterday: An Informal History of the Nineteen-Twenties* (New York: Blue Ribbon Books, Inc. 1931),165.

Dot, at age 14, the only child at home. We don't know how that affected her, but we can assume that the role made her increasingly independent and probably more assertive. She entered ninth grade that fall when the older brothers went off to college.

At Carthage College, Gene followed the pattern of his older brothers by displaying excellence on the athletic field as well as in the classroom. For example, he received one grade of A and the rest A+ grades in the last semester of his senior year. He majored in chemistry, intending to go on to medical school. Though always modest about his accomplishments, his football career involved one significant brush with history.

Carthage belonged to the Little Nineteen athletics conference. One rival was Eureka College, also a small liberal arts college located north and east of Carthage. In the Carthage College *Collegian* for November 16, 1928, the headline on page 1 read: "Redmen Hold Eureka at 7-0 in First Victory of Season." The Carthage eleven played at Eureka in mud, rain, and sleet.

They were in the middle of their football season. Hub was assistant coach; Gene the star fullback. Despite the inclement weather, the Carthage boys performed well against the Eureka Tornadoes. In particular, fullback Gene Wagner "hit the line like a bullet and punted as only Gene can punt." In the opinion of the reporter, "It was a great day and a great game."

The next year the two foes met November 15 on the Carthage field. Going into the final minutes of the 1929 game, Carthage fans thought they would surely be victorious. Again, the account of what happened next comes from the *Collegian* for November 15. Gene had scored the only touchdown for Carthage in the first quarter. They led 7-0. Carthage fans sat on the edge of their seats as Gene punted to Eureka's 25-yard line. Next came what the fans thought was the break of the game for them. Eureka threw a "wild, desperate, last minute attempt pass" that fell into the hands of one of their guards at mid-field, after "being batted and fumbled by everyone, including the drum major, it seemed like." The Eureka guard who found himself in possession of the ball proceeded to run fifty yards to the goal line; a minute later a drop-kick split the uprights.

Wait a minute! A guard is an ineligible pass receiver. Was the ball dead or alive when caught? "Opinions as to the legality of the pass were many and diversified." There were no cameras in that era to provide instant replay for the referees to look at in double-checking their decisions. However, the officials finally ruled that the play was legal, and the game ended in a 7-7 tie. Carthage fans undoubtedly thought they had been robbed.

Gene's brush with history was not known for a few decades. When the Eureka guard who caught the fumbled "wild, desperate" pass graduated from college, he landed a job as sports commentator for WOC radio in Davenport. From there he advanced to Des Moines, then Hollywood, Sacramento, and eventually the White House. That Eureka guard, who cost Carthage a victory, was none other than Ronald Reagan.

Gene graduated from college in June 1931, performed day labor during the summer, and taught school in a small southern Illinois town for the next three years until he had enough money to attend medical school.

Aunt Dot had graduated from Davenport High School in January 1931 and had gone to work. She may have been skipped ahead a grade like her brothers or she may have taken extra credits in prior semesters. In any event, Aunt Dot had to go to work. The Depression had hit everyone in 1929. For the Wagner family, the hard times had started in 1928, when Aunt Dot was a sophomore in high school. A look back at what happened to the family gives us a picture of the lessons in resilience that Aunt Dot would have learned during her high school years.

Notes

- A biography of Fred Wagner, in a 1910 history of Cedar County, Iowa, details more of the German immigrant's "dominant characteristics of ambition and industry." Within the seven years since he had purchased a "wild, undeveloped tract" of land, Fred brought his acreage into a "high state of cultivation." He also built a large house, barn, and outbuildings. By 1910, he was ranked "among the substantial and representative farmers" of his township.[10] Clearly, Grandpa had inherited and cultivated those same characteristics that his older brother displayed.

- The Staubitz Archive at Carthage College and the Registrar's Office provided transcripts for the Wagner family and for August Gruhn, as well as copies of the student paper cited above and the college yearbook, then called the *Crimson Rambler*.

- Pictures from the *Rambler*, as well as my own recollections, provided the basis for my descriptions of the campus and the town. I lived in Carthage until age 7, when Hub no longer taught and coached at the college.

---

[10] C. Ray Aurner, ed., *A Topical History of Cedar County Iowa*, vol. 2 (Chicago: S.J. Clarke Publishing Company, 1910), 233-4.

The entrance to Carthage College, as shown in the 1933 annual, the Crimson Rambler.

The Field House was dedicated on January 16, 1931, according to college historians. Over 500 alumni and townspeople attended the ceremonies, at which the Commissioner of the Big Ten spoke. With two gymnasiums and theater seats on one side, the building accommodated the entire college population for convocations, graduation, and worship.

In this photo, Aunt Dot is wearing the same dress as in her high school photo, but she is not wearing glasses. Perhaps this picture was taken when when she went to Carthage College in 1932.

CHAPTER THREE

Choices

One's mettle is tested when disaster strikes a family. Choices made can have a lasting impact. Very likely such choices depend upon immediate circumstances as well as the family members' prior experience and their psychological strength. For example, are they strong or weak? Hard worker or lazy? Persistent or erratic? When financial disaster descended on the Wagner family in 1928, all of the members at home pitched in and contributed to common, as well as individual, goals that were both immediate and long range.

The prosperity of the 1920s throughout the country, as well as the death of a company president, probably led to the complete merger of Harned and VonMaur with J.H.C Petersen Company in downtown Davenport. According to the company's history, the two had been operating as separate stores but under common ownership since 1916. But on May 7, 1928, the merger occurred, creating one store known as Petersen Harned Von Maur. "The buildings that had housed Harned and Von Maur were leased to a company from New York, and operations moved into the former Petersen store." Ultimately, this merger left Grandpa, who had been managing Department A Company on the fifth floor of Harned and Von Maur, with a stock of merchandise in a defunct store, in a closed building.

In his retirement years, Hub wrote the story of Grandpa's work history for us cousins. According to Hub's recounting, sometime after the stores' merger, Grandpa was forced to rent a small space on ground level to liquidate his merchandise. In Hub's own words: "When he had finished liquidating his stock, he had lost everything but the home." Grandpa was 54 years old. Efforts to find similar work failed; he was considered too old.

To have built up a department, gained controlling interest, and then become the victim of decisions made by others would have been devastating, especially since this was the second time in twelve years that Grandpa had incurred such a business loss. In some ways, it is easier to face a disaster if you can realize it is your own fault. But to think that you have done everything right, and then to become an innocent victim of others' actions, feels unjust and physically like being kicked in the gut. Hub recalled that one night he and Gene went out looking for Grandpa when he did not come home for supper. Hub found him sitting on a bench in Vander Veer Park, looking totally dejected. We don't know what was said. We do know that Grandpa, unlike his father decades earlier in Germany, did not turn to drink. He looked for work.

In an era when families ate their meals together and talked over the dinner table, the entire Wagner family, during that summer and fall of 1928, would have suffered emotionally as well as financially with the loss of Grandpa's job. Grandma may have been the strongest one in terms of daily activity. She would have remembered financial struggles when her father, Claus Stoltenberg, had been laid up for weeks at a time with illness. She would have remembered going to work herself as a domestic at age 13, to help bring money home to the family. Like an anchor, Grandma would have kept on with her familiar daily role—cleaning the house, keeping the family's clothes clean and mended, preparing three meals daily, and baking weekly. If the food budget was excessively lean, Grandma knew how to prepare a meal with brains and gizzard for protein. According to Hub's written account, Grandpa took any job he could get and that he was physically able to handle. Hub and Gene, home from Carthage College for the summer, worked at day labor to help the family treasury. But Gene also had to save for three more years of college tuition, room, and board. Whether or not there was talk of him dropping out of college, we do not know. Hub had been earning a salary as a faculty member at the college, but only for one year. However, his job was secure for the coming year. At age 15, we don't know what work Aunt Dot could have gotten. She may have hired out to clean homes as Grandma had done in her youth.

Little did the Wagners know that, before long, others in Davenport would also be facing financial disaster and ruin. In less than two years, the entire country was plunged into the worst depression in its history. But before that debacle, in the remaining months of 1928 and during the first half of the next year, the market climbed to astonishing heights. In the words of popular chronicler Frederick Lewis Allen, "During most of 1928 and 1929 buying stocks was like betting at a race track at which, fantastically, most of the horses won."[11]

---

[11] Frederick Lewis Allen, *The Big Change: America Transforms Itself 1900-1950* (New York: Harper & Brothers Publishers, 1952), 142.

But in the fall of 1929, the stock market faltered, then recovered. Still, there were jitters. No one really knew what was going on. The market had ascended to such dizzying heights that people assumed it would always keep going up and up. New York bankers tried to infuse more money into the market to help stem the tide of buying; too many people were buying on margin. But nothing seemed to work. People on Wall Street had seen the daily fluctuations all fall. "On the worst day, October 29, over sixteen million shares of stock were thrown on the market by frantic sellers. And it was not until November 13 that order was restored."[12] That was merely a temporary lull. A volatile market eventually crashed. What has come to be known as the Great Depression blanketed the nation. The effect was not temporary but lasting. In her history of Davenport, Marlys Svendsen notes that by 1932 thousands were on relief. By 1933, more than half the manufacturing force had been laid off in this city of over 60,000 residents. Fifty companies closed. Many others cut back on the number of employees. "The value of wages dropped to . . . less than half its 1929 peak."[13] Banks failed in Iowa and around the country.

The Wagner family found themselves in company with much of the city's and country's population—although the Wagners had lost everything sometime in 1928 while the rest of the people suffered from 1929 on. The country's economy lagged throughout the decade of the 1930s. There were no government programs as we know them today, so people simply had to make do as best they could. Pictures from the decade show men lined up for bread and soup—lines that stretched for city blocks. In the worst cases, there were stories of people, unable to face catastrophe, committing suicide. The effect on the country was psychological as well as financial. Writing in 1931, Frederick Lewis Allen summed up the nation's climate:

> The Big Bull Market had been more than the climax of a business cycle; it had been the climax of a cycle in American mass thinking and mass emotion. There was hardly a man or woman in the country whose attitude toward life had not been affected by the sudden and brutal shattering of hope. With the Big Bull Market gone and prosperity going, Americans were soon to find themselves living in an altered world which called for new adjustments, new ideas, new habits

---

[12] Allen, *The Big Change*, 145.
[13] Svendsen, 130.

of thought and a new order of values. The psychological climate was changing. . . .[14]

Despite having "lost everything" but their house, the Wagners did not succumb to prolonged depression or worse. From what we cousins know, and from what public documents tell us, the family members kept working and studying. In the face of daily hardship, they did not give up on their long-term goals.

We do not know how the decision was arrived at, but one strategic choice the Wagners made was to remodel the Brady Street house so that the downstairs could be rented out and, thus, some income could be received each month. Hub never told us about the cost of such re-modeling, and the Davenport Library has no records for it. We do know that Hub loaned his parents money for the project, since he was single and still earning a paycheck at Carthage College. Hardt no longer lived in Davenport. He had been married in 1925 and was teaching at South Dakota State University; so he had a wife to support, and the future of his job was not clear.

From the addresses in the Davenport *City Directory*, it seems that the remodeling occurred sometime between summer and fall of 1930 and one year later. According to the Special Collections staff of the Davenport Library, data for the *City Directory* were gathered in April of the year of publication. The Wagners' address in the 1930 *City Directory* reads 2925 Brady Street. Their address in the 1931 *City Directory* reads 2925½ Brady Street.

In effect, what the family did was to add on to both the first and second floors—including a new bedroom and bathroom on each floor. In addition, the original bathroom on the second floor became Grandma's new kitchen. Enclosed back stairs had to be added so Grandma could go down two flights of stairs to the basement for washing clothes. Grandma also had to accommodate herself to a much smaller kitchen—no counter space except a small table, no cupboards, and a small stove. The former bathroom linen closet became her pantry for dishes and pans. Aunt Dot would still have had her own bedroom. The brothers would have had to sleep in the attic whenever they were home from college, because the front bedroom became a living room, and the remaining bedroom became a dining room. Presumably, Grandpa and Grandma chose to live

---

[14] Allen, *Only Yesterday*, 338.

in the upstairs apartment, so that they had the added space of the attic for both sleeping and storage. Probably they also could command more rent for a downstairs apartment.

For those at home during the summer and fall of 1930 when the construction was underway, daily life would have been stressful. Noise, dust, and ever-changing traffic patterns with construction materials lying around house and yard would have created daily inconveniences, to say nothing of workmen under foot. Grandma, as the only person who worked solely in the home, would have suffered the most. According to the 1930 census, Grandpa worked as a "census-taker." Gene's occupation was listed as "janitor" for a "college gymnasium." That was probably his job during the school year. During the summer, he would have worked as a day-laborer in Davenport. Hub was recorded on the census schedule as a teacher, but he took the bus to Ann Arbor, Michigan, for graduate study in the summer of 1930. By that time, Hardt and his wife were back there, and he was again pursuing his Ph.D. studies while teaching part-time at the university. The Ann Arbor *Directory* says they were living with his in-laws.

The federal census reports that Aunt Dot worked in Davenport as a "saleslady" at the "Ten cent store." The term referred to stores, also called the dime store or the five and dime, which had been around for more than fifty years. The Woolworth Brothers first pioneered the concept of a variety store in Pennsylvania. Moving west, the Brothers maintained their five and ten cent prices until the spring of 1932 when they added a twenty cent line of merchandise. Davenport had a Woolworth Store located on West Second Street, where there was also another famous dime store chain run by the Kresge Co. For Aunt Dot to have gotten a job at the "Ten cent store" in downtown Davenport would indicate that she proved reliable, able to meet the public in an agreeable manner, and could handle money efficiently as well as make out sales slips.

Since the census was taken in April, Aunt Dot probably worked part time while still in school. She would have turned 17 in February 1930 and looked forward to completing her senior year at Davenport High School in the fall. As the only sibling at home during the entire year, it seems likely that Aunt Dot experienced first hand the stresses that her parents were under during the weeks of renovation. She could not have forgotten about the experience in later years.

Given Grandpa's business loss just before her first year in high school, plus the onset of the Depression, it seems fair to say that Aunt

Dot's high school years would have been filled with study, work, and church. She would very probably have made her own clothes, perhaps with Grandma's help. That might have resulted in some mother-daughter squabbles. Grandma always made her own dresses; she wore them long with her hemlines about ten inches above the floor, as had been the style during the World War I years. She also wore cotton stockings held up by a corset. But the image of young women had changed dramatically in the 1920s when Aunt Dot was growing into her teen years. The "with it" female of that decade wore her skirts shortened to the knees; silk stockings rolled down to the knee; no corset, thin slip, and long-waisted dress. A boyishly slim figure became the ideal. On top of this skimpy costume, the "flapper" bobbed her hair, wore rouge and lipstick, and smoked and drank with the men if she wanted. Aunt Dot may have aspired to such attire, but she would not have smoked, taken liquor, or frequented a speakeasy. She had been raised in a dry household and certainly knew that selling or drinking liquor was against the law. Moreover, she would not have been in social situations where she even was tempted. However, growing up in Davenport was far from existing in a reclusive atmosphere.

Despite the Depression economy, Davenport had not come to a standstill. The 1931 *City Directory* gives an extensive "Statistical Review," which includes the following data: Five railroads carried passengers and freight in and out of the city. The population numbered 60,751 residents, according to the federal census of 1930. Ninety percent of those residents were American-born. People lived in 15,475 homes, about 75 percent of which were owned by the occupants. Connecting folks were 18,448 telephones, all of which functioned with the skill and friendly voices of female operators. Dial service was not installed until 1935.[15] Two daily papers plus the radio brought national and local news, sports, music, and soap operas to city residents. Vander Veer Park was just one of thirteen city parks, encompassing over 700 acres. Pastors in forty-eight churches, of all denominations, ministered to the spiritual needs of the community. Perhaps sometimes rivaling the churches, Davenport had fourteen theaters with a total seating capacity of 9,100 persons.

By 1930, sound had been synchronized with pictures for only three years. Talking, singing, and instrumental ensembles like big bands were huge attractions on stage and on screen. But the era also was filled with gangland killings, bootleg liquor, bank robberies, and racketeering. An

---

[15] Svendsen, 81.

advertisement in the *Davenport Daily Times* for January 7, 1930, makes the point. The RKO Capitol was showing *The Racketeer*, starring Robert Armstrong with Carol Lombard, described as "A Thrilling All-Talking Romance of the Underworld." A harmonica band was featured live on stage between showings.

We can assume that Aunt Dot went to the movies once in a while with friends. Admission to movies in 1930 averaged twenty-five cents, according to the Davenport Library. But Aunt Dot would not have followed the antics of Gene when he was at Carthage College. In later years, he told us cousins that he and his buddies would occasionally sneak into the back door of the Woodbine Theater in Carthage and watch the movie in reverse image. They simply had no money to pay for admission by the front entrance. He never told us whether or not Mrs. Girard, the owner, ever caught them sneaking in or not.

Aunt Dot finished Davenport High School in the mid-year graduation ceremony for 1931. Pictures of the senior class of Davenport High School show that ninety-five students graduated in January; the remainder in June. Altogether 309 students comprised the total graduating class. Aunt Dot finished in January, just a few weeks before she turned 18. Out of forty-six women who graduated in mid-year, Aunt Dot was the only one who wore glasses in her senior picture. Glasses in that era were not flattering; round lenses with dark black frames could make one look rather owlish. Whether she was self-conscious about her appearance we have no way of knowing. But one thing we know for sure, the images of women in her high school class of 1931 did not resemble the "flapper" of the 1920s. Just as the hemlines went up with the market rise of the twenties, hemlines came down when the market crashed at the start of the thirties. Conservatism had taken over female fashions. Pictures of the women in Aunt Dot's class show short, softly curled hair but not the extreme, saucy bobs of the previous decade. Headshots suggest modest and tailored, not flamboyant, feminine images.

Aunt Dot must have had a pleasing personality and made friends easily. Each senior's picture carried a descriptive quote beneath it. "Smiles are the language of love" accompanied Aunt Dot's picture. Other captions indicated that she belonged to the French Club, Glee Club, and Chorus. She also served as secretary of the Student Club. She followed a program of study called the General Course. Just over 46 percent of the total class completed the General Course. Other options included the Normal Course, the Latin Course, the Commercial Course, the Science

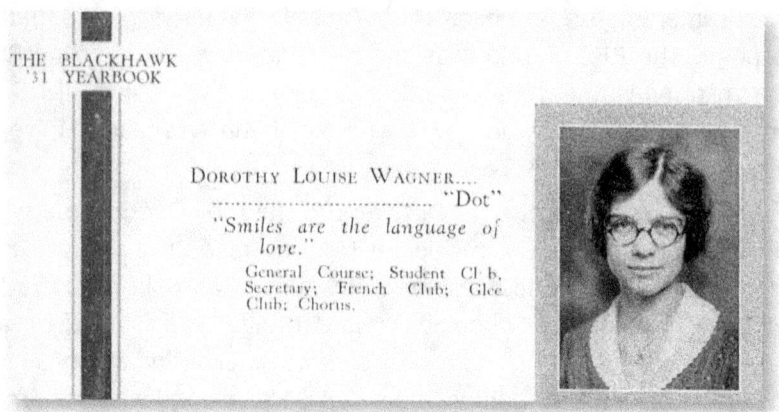

Dot's entry in the 1931 Davenport High School Yearbook.

Course, and the Manual Training Course. Aunt Dot's curriculum would not have prepared her exclusively for college, but she was prepared for higher education. The Director of the Davenport School Museum said that the General Course was the curriculum pursued if a student was undecided about his or her future. In the case of Aunt Dot, her courses included skills in stenographic work as well as traditional academic study. By contrast, the Commercial Course would have focused exclusively on stenography, bookkeeping, accounting, and the like.

The fact that Aunt Dot did not pursue the Commercial Course suggests that she had college in mind for the future. She certainly had the example of three older brothers who had not only finished college, but also were progressing toward multiple graduate degrees. Gene was teaching and saving for medical school. In the summer of 1931, Hub began his annual bus rides to New York City to enter Columbia University and begin his second master's degree, this one in physical education. At the same time, Hardt was continuing to pursue the Ph.D. degree in mathematics at the University of Michigan, while teaching part-time at the university in order to pay for his expenses.

Although we do not know what her parents thought of a woman going on to college, Aunt Dot certainly had a strong influence from her brothers. In addition, Gene's daughter Nancy recalls her father recounting once that the brothers promised Grandpa they would help Aunt Dot go to college if they could. By contrast, Aunt Dot had no female influence from cousins or aunts who had attended college. We have no statistics from the Davenport Library or School Museum about the number of women from the 1931 class who went on to college.

What we do know for sure is that Aunt Dot worked as a stenographer for the United States Hospital Supply Company in downtown Davenport. The 1932 *City Directory* lists her in this position, but she may have begun in that employment right after graduation and continued in it for about a year-and-a-half until she did indeed enroll in Carthage College in the fall of 1932. But before that date, she would have heard news of her older brother and the effect of the Depression on the college itself.

The *Carthage College Alumnus*, March 15, 1932, carried a front-page column by the President, Jacob Diehl, about the criteria for selecting a good college. The front page also carried a lengthy article about the basketball team winning the Little Nineteen championship. Hub had been coaching the team since 1927 and brought the college its first such championship. The detailed article, naming players, statistics, and opponents, carried a by-line of the *Chicago Tribune*, March 8. The third front-page feature was a "Letter from Dean Torgeson." As the new Dean of Women, Olive Torgeson urged contributions from alumni so that the women students in Denhart Hall could have a more livable environment:

> We have three parlors, a large reception hall, and a library in Denhart Hall. In these five rooms we have one floor lamp and one table lamp. I am sure that in most of our homes we consider these lamps a necessity and that we have wall and floor sockets in every room. Some of the things the girls would like to have this year are more lamps for our parlors, some occasional tables to give a more home-like atmosphere, and light sockets so that we need not have a network of light cords in each room.

She goes on to say that the girls would also like to have more furniture and a radio in the parlor so that they could listen to musical programs and entertain their guests more comfortably. Further, she writes of the recent banquet held in the Denhart dining room, celebrating the basketball championship. "It was a joyous occasion and the room with its tables decorated in the college colors, was lovely." However, she notes that to have more of such events, the college required new table linens, silver, and eventually new dishes. Thus, her letter is a plea for money at a time when money was very, very scarce.

Olive Torgeson began her tenure as Dean of Women in January 1932. She had previously worked for six years as assistant university examiner in the Office of the Registrar at the University of Iowa, where she was earning a salary of $2,000 per year. In later years, long after she had become my mother, she told me that, at an opening tea that January, one of the Carthage College faculty wives said to her, "Well you know, don't you, that they are not paying salaries." My mother said her heart sank. She had been supporting herself and sending money home each month to her widowed mother. No doubt my mother wondered about the decision she had made in taking on this new position. I never heard any more of her doubts or worries.

She, Hub, and the other faculty carried on with their work and simply made do, figuring that was their only choice, given the state of the nation's economy. Celebrating the college's first basketball championship was cause for rejoicing in a year that held little else to celebrate. Historians of the college note that the board of trustees had invested too much of the school's endowment in real estate. The Depression brought disaster to the endowment. Foreclosures abounded. Fewer students entered the college. Many who entered could not pay their bills. They worked and were carried on the books if they stayed in school. Faculty went without a paycheck for several months. Single faculty could eat at the Denhart Hall dining room. Faculty with families could get meat and produce from the college's kitchen and farms. No one, of course, bought clothes or went to the dentist or did anything else that cost money. Hub and another single man rented rooms in town; they had one dollar between them. Whoever went out carried the dollar bill.

Somehow Hub had managed to save some money from summer labor and previous paychecks so that he could ride the bus again to New York City for summer school at Columbia University in 1932. He told us in later years that entertainment consisted of sitting in on the night police court. That was free. In Michigan, Hardt had been teaching part-time, in addition to completing his dissertation. He received his Ph.D. in mathematics in June 1932. After a year or so, he secured a job as an actuarial clerk. In southern Illinois, Gene hitchhiked home from his teaching job at the start of summer and worked day labor to continue saving for medical school.

At the same time, Grandpa's perseverance eventually began to pay off. Hub's work history says that after a couple of years, Grandpa found employment with a former competitor, the Folwell China Company. Though paid very little, he became a trusted employee and was often sent to other cities to fill in for the company on a temporary basis. His work for Folwell's lasted for twenty years. Eventually he again became a manager. His salary, together with their rental income, gave Grandpa and Grandma a sufficient livelihood in their later years.

We know from Carthage College records that Aunt Dot enrolled in the fall of 1932. It seems that the power of family tradition made it a foregone conclusion that she would follow in the footsteps of her older brothers. Given Grandpa's business loss and the onset of the Depression, we can assume that Aunt Dot had to work and save for her expenses. The costs seem very small compared to today, but at the time college expenses were proportionate to the total economy and money was hard to come by. The Carthage College catalogue for 1932-33 says that room charges varied between $50 and $60. Board cost $195, tuition $180, and books from $25-35. For her first year in college, Aunt Dot would have had to pay between $450 and $475.

Given the hard economic times, the small number of students at Carthage is hardly surprising. Men outnumbered women, and attrition set in as students progressed from first year to final year. In the fall of 1932, Aunt Dot was one of forty-four women who enrolled. Fifty-three men complemented the females. The senior class for that year of 1932-33 consisted of thirty-three men and only thirteen women. Altogether 288 men and women comprised the student body.

Aunt Dot's transcript indicates that in her freshman year she took two semesters each of chemistry, French, and English plus one semester of Old Testament. It also suggests that she was headed toward a home economics major, since she had completed two semesters of clothing and one semester of home nursing. In her sophomore year, she continued with the home economics courses, including two semesters of art and design, one semester of foods, and one semester of childcare. For her general courses, she again took two semesters each of French and English, one semester of chemistry, one semester of Bible, and two semesters of philosophy. For her physical education courses, Aunt Dot selected two semesters each of archery and tap dancing. There were no competitive sports for women in the 1930s, and the transcript does not indicate if she participated in intramurals. In an era when grade inflation was unknown and a grade of C was considered average, Aunt Dot had no grades of C recorded on her transcript. Unlike her older brothers, she received no grades of A+. However, she incurred only two grades of B-; the remainder of her grades were almost evenly divided between B and A.

Aunt Dot, thus, proved to have the intellectual capacity for study that her brothers possessed, but she had no opportunity for intercollegiate athletics as they did. Their college days had been devoted to study and sports, with a small but unknown amount of social life, though no steady girl friends. By contrast, Aunt Dot's time, typical of girls then in college, would have been spent on study and social life. Carthage College had local, not national, sororities and fraternities. There were also choir concerts and clubs focused on special interests, e.g. the Dramatic Club. Not least, there were football and basketball games to attend. In addition, two Christian organizations contributed to the religious and devotional life of students. At the beginning of each school year, the YWCA sponsored an event for new freshmen to meet upper-class students. And annually, faculty sponsored a reception in Denhart Hall for freshmen and new students. Throughout the year, various other kinds of all-college affairs took place. Though many church colleges at that time did not allow coed dancing on campus, Carthage had proved more liberal a few years before by permitting dancing. One college historian, writing in 1945, noted that spring formals brought out "male chivalry and feminine beauty" in "full dress parade."[16] Given the small student population and the small, compact physical space of the campus, it is clear that Aunt Dot would have had ample opportunity to meet senior student August Gruhn during her first year at Carthage in 1932-33.

Gruhn had followed in the wake of his older brother, Harold, by entering Carthage after six years in a Missouri Synod Lutheran high school and associated junior college in Milwaukee. According to August Gruhn's transcript, he entered Carthage College with advanced standing on February 10, 1932. He graduated with a bachelor's degree on June 5, 1933. His transcript does not list a major.

Looking at his courses, it appears that he was studying music; the transcript includes one credit of college choir in addition to harmony and voice. His transcript does not list participation in athletics, although in a later biography he indicates that he earned a letter in track as a distance runner.

Social mores required that boys ask the girls out for a date; the reverse did not hold true. Since Gruhn belonged to a fraternity, he might have asked Aunt Dot to one of the fraternity's social events. Perhaps to a play or a concert. Lack of money would not have hampered social activities because much was available right on campus. Since he was three years older and a senior, Aunt Dot may have been "swept off her

---

[16] Spielman, 137.

GRUHN, AUGUST   Milwaukee, Wis.
"Direct not him, whose way himself
    will choose;
'Tis breath thou lack'st, and that
    breath wilt thou lose."
Richard II, Act II, Scene 1.

From the Carthage Crimson Rambler. Dot met August Gruhn when he was a senior and she was a first year student at Carthage College.

feet." The recommendations for Gruhn to enter the chaplaincy, as noted in chapter one, tout him as having a "pleasing" and "commanding" personality. If Aunt Dot's experience of dating had been very limited, she may have been thrilled and flattered to be asked out by an upperclassman. We can only guess at the frequency of their contact, but social mores also dictated that their times together were public occasions; telephone talks would have been minimal to absent. Very likely, telephones in the girl's dormitory numbered only one per floor.

Aunt Dot returned to Carthage College as a sophomore student during the 1933-34 academic year. Gruhn went to Minneapolis and enrolled in Northwestern Lutheran Seminary, again following in the wake of his older brother. We can speculate that Aunt Dot and Gruhn wrote letters back and forth. Long distance telephone calls would have been out of the question due to cost. We can also speculate that they must have had an understanding. Aunt Dot withdrew from Carthage on June 4, 1934. For her to have left school and followed him to Minneapolis without some kind of understanding that would lead to marriage suggests that she was flouting familial and Lutheran norms as well as midwestern, middle class social tradition. I think that was not true. Still, within the family, her action made her something of a quiet rebel.

Several factors could have affected Aunt Dot's decision to leave school. Money was still tight. Her entering class of women at Carthage had already declined from forty-four to thirty-nine women by the start of their sophomore year. Whether or not to return for their junior year of college would have been a hot topic among the girls in Denhart Hall. Could they earn enough during summers to pay for another school year's expenses? Did they want to take on more debt? If girls had a realistic prospect of marriage, they might have thought that was the most sensible path to follow. Aunt Dot had grown up in a home where her parents respected each other and contributed equally to the well-being of the household. Marriage and family were clearly the ideal toward which young women of that era strived. Aunt Dot's transcript implies she intended to major in home economics, a further focus on home and family. She may also have been affected by Hub's behavior on the small college campus

When the young bachelor basketball coach began visiting the young Dean of Women in the Denhart Hall parlors, there is no doubt that the buzz spread rapidly around campus. In addition to her duties as Dean of Women, Olive Torgeson also taught a sociology course in the college's Department of History and Social Science. So the two were teaching colleagues in the same department. Carthage records indicate that Olive Torgeson resigned as Dean of Women in June 1934. The girls of Denhart Hall, including Aunt Dot, gave her a pendant, which she wore a year later, on June 26, 1935, as her only wedding jewelry. The courtship between two young faculty members would have seemed romantic to the residents in Denhart Hall. They may also have thought that Aunt Dot's decision was rather romantic as well.

Within the Wagner family, Grandma probably thought that marriage to a minister was a goal worth pursuing. By contrast, Grandpa could well have been disappointed. Aunt Dot's leaving school to follow a young man may have reminded Grandpa of his younger sister, Caroline Louise. She had emigrated with her mother at the age of 11. Both then lived with oldest son and brother, Fred, on his farm north of Davenport. To have accomplished all that he did since emigrating, Fred would have managed home and family with an iron hand. Caroline Louise is listed in the 1900 census as living on the farm, but she rebelled at that life. Sometime after that year, she ran off with one George Haman. They married in Texas in 1903. By the 1910 census, she had four children. Subsequently, she abandoned her husband and children, according to oral family history. She occasionally sent post cards to Grandpa from out west. Aunt Dot and Caroline Louise were both the only girls with three older, strong-minded, and ambitious brothers. One wonders about family patterns. Was alcohol a factor?

To reject college for marriage to a bright prospect—especially a Lutheran minister—could hardly be considered an ill-advised decision. Aunt Dot was simply operating within the cultural ideal for women in the 1930s. On the other hand, her choice to sacrifice her own college education in order to be near her future husband points up the gender differences of the era. Women looked forward to marriage, home, and family with little to no thought of a career outside the home. By contrast, men took it for granted that they were entitled to it all—education, career, marriage, home, and family.

What we do not know about Aunt Dot's choice is the degree to which she made the choice of her own free will and/or the degree to which Gruhn strongly persuaded her to move to Minneapolis. Recalling again the fact that one of Gruhn's references for entry into the chaplaincy said he had a "commanding" personality, we can assume that he spoke persuasively in favor of Aunt Dot leaving college and moving to Minneapolis. And she may have heard his entreaties with the heart of a woman who was young, inexperienced, and filled with romantic dreams of marriage and family rather than duty, discipline, and education.

Aunt Dot came naturally by her courage, spirit of adventure, and pursuit of a dream, when considering Grandpa's early choices, i.e. emigrating by himself and then returning ten years later to see the World's Fair all by himself. Moreover, her two older brothers had left Davenport for New York City and Ann Arbor, Michigan, albeit they were both pursuing graduate degrees. For Aunt Dot to follow Gruhn when she probably didn't even have a ring was perhaps also considered unseemly by family members. However, money was very tight; Gruhn had been a student and, undoubtedly, earning money for his college and seminary expenses. It would not have been unusual for seminary students and their intended to simply have an understanding. Such an agreement was understood in clerical circles to be extremely serious. The Lutheran seminaries of that era wanted their students to be single while studying for the ministry but to be married when they received their first call to a congregation. According to one historical account, if a seminarian broke his engagement, it could be grounds for being thrown out of the seminary.[17]

We have no way of knowing how Aunt Dot got herself settled in Minneapolis. We might assume that she travelled by bus to the city, because it would have been cheaper than train travel. We also have no way of knowing how she found a place to live and a job. It seems unlikely that

---

[17] Gracia Grindal, "The Role of Women in Seminary Life," in *Thanksgiving and Hope: A collection of essays chronicling 125 years of the people, events and movements in the antecedent schools that have formed Luther Seminary*, ed. Frederick H. Gonnerman (St. Paul: Luther Seminary, 1998), 87.

Gruhn would have been much help since he lived at the seminary building which was located in north Minneapolis, a long distance from where Aunt Dot first rented. The *City Directory* for 1934-35 lists Dorothy L. Wagner as residing at 3030 Harriett Avenue South and working at the big Sears Roebuck store. Driving by that address today, we see a single family dwelling of about two stories. Judging by its architecture and apparent age, it is undoubtedly the same house in which Aunt Dot lived. It is located on a residential street one block south of Lake Street, a main thoroughfare, and several blocks west of the Sears store. Streetcars would have provided easy access for Aunt Dot to get to the store. Chances are that she simply went to the store and applied for a job. Given that she had had experience working as a "saleslady" at the "ten cent store" and as a stenographer at the Hospital Supply Co., she could certainly have produced references.

The Sears store, the tower of which was visible for blocks around, had opened in March 1928 and served as the centerpiece of a thriving mid-town business district during the middle decades of the twentieth century. According to the company's history, the building served both retail and mail order business, and employed some 2,000 workers at any one point in time. Though the economy was still tight in 1934, it seems probable that Aunt Dot had little difficulty in securing a job. She was 21 years old with the poise and maturity that came from prior work experience plus two years of college.

Her living accommodations at the Harriett Avenue address would have been modest. Typical of the era, Aunt Dot would have rented a room and probably shared a bathroom; she may have had kitchen privileges or been permitted to keep a hotplate in her room. Having a full apartment would have been costly and not usual for a young single girl at that time. Whether the arrangement proved unsatisfactory or another place sounded better, we do not know. But after one year she moved to a north Minneapolis address, which was a lot farther from work at the Sears store and no closer to the seminary where Gruhn lived and studied.

The next year she moved again, this time to an address in south Minneapolis within easy walking distance to the Sears store. The *City Directories* for 1936 and for 1937 indicate that she remained at this Park Avenue house for two years. Driving by the residence at 3140 Park Avenue today, it is clear that the house is very likely the same one in which Aunt Dot roomed. It appears to be a three-story dwelling located two blocks south of Lake Street and three blocks west of the Sears store. Aunt Dot probably still rented a room but could have had her own bathroom, given the apparent size of the house. Although this address remained the same for two years, Aunt Dot did not have her own telephone. A search of the Minneapolis telephone directories from 1934 through 1937 has no listing for Dorothy or Dorothy L. Wagner.

The *City Directory* for 1937 suggests that Aunt Dot may have gotten a promotion at work. She is listed as employed by Sears Roebuck and Co. in the preceding directories. But in 1937, she is listed as a stenographer. That would have been a skilled job. One would assume that such a position paid more than that of a saleslady.

We have no way of knowing what kind of social life Aunt Dot had. Certainly, she could have met other working girls at the Sears store and possibly even at the Park Avenue residence, since the dwelling looks sufficiently large to have had more than one renter. Aunt Dot could also have met other women through church. She might have joined a church choir since she sang in the choir and glee club at Davenport High School. But it seems probable that her time with Gruhn would have been the most important social time on her calendar.

However, trying to figure out how often Aunt Dot and Gruhn got together for social occasions or just to share a meal is difficult to estimate. Not least, he lived at the seminary, and that address was a long way from where Aunt Dot lived and worked. According to the *Seminary Bulletin* for January 1933, Northwestern Lutheran Theological Seminary was housed in what today looks like an unpretentious two-story brick building at 1018 19th Avenue N.E. in Minneapolis. It was "within twelve minutes ride on the street car from the business district of Minneapolis, and within fifteen minutes ride from the University of Minnesota." The building accommodated "all the needs of the school," including a gymnasium with showers.[18] Thus, all of Gruhn's daily life as a seminary student took place in this single building nineteen blocks north of the downtown business area. The Sears store was another thirty blocks south of the downtown area. Although the streetcar system was well-developed by the mid-thirties, still it would have taken time for Gruhn and Aunt Dot to get together for a date.

Northwestern Seminary was small in terms of student population and also conservative, though not extremely so, as evidenced by the fact that Gruhn became a youth pastor at a Methodist church while he was finishing his final seminary degree. The school's official statement

---

[18] *Northwestern Seminary Bulletin* 9 (January 1933): 7.

in their *Bulletin* said: "The policy of this seminary is to foster sound and conservative Lutheranism and to work in harmony and co-operation with all who labor toward the same end." Five faculty members taught a total of twenty-four students.[19] When Gruhn enrolled in the fall of 1933, his older brother Harold would have been a senior.

To receive the Bachelor of Divinity degree, students completed one of two standard curricula. The difference being that one course included Hebrew and Greek while the other permitted the study of the Old and New Testaments in the English language. Either of these curricula required three years of study. A post-graduate course granted the degree Master of Sacred Theology. August Gruhn earned both the B.D. and the S.T.M. degrees in the requisite four years of study. In addition, he gained experience by serving as a student assistant at St. Olaf's Lutheran Church in north Minneapolis from 1933 to 1935. According to Gruhn's own biography written in later years, he served as a youth pastor at Wesley Methodist Church in downtown Minneapolis from 1935 to 1937. That would have been a part-time position that probably paid some salary as well as providing experience.

The *Seminary Bulletin* also says that the academic year consisted of six terms of five weeks each. It doesn't say how those terms were distributed throughout the calendar year, nor does it say anything about vacation times. Given their study, work, and time consumed in public transportation, it seems that Aunt Dot and Gruhn might have shared a meal or a movie once in a while. Certainly they would have attended special events or celebrations at the seminary. For example, the *Seminary Bulletin* for April 1935 says that the students gave an annual Christmas party in honor of their faculty. A dinner followed a "social evening" with a "full complement of ladies" in attendance.[20] Despite many unknowns, one thing remains abundantly clear; Gruhn and Aunt Dot would have had little to no private time together, given the social mores of the day and the strict moral code imposed on the seminary students. He could not have visited her living quarters; she could not have visited his. Any times they shared as a couple would have been in a public space.

Articles in the *Minneapolis Star Tribune* suggest that Aunt Dot became active in the two congregations where Gruhn was serving. One picture from May 1935 shows the two of them, plus other young people, grouped around a table working on some plans for an upcoming Lutheran Youth

---

[19] Ibid., 6-7.
[20] *Northwestern Seminary Bulletin* 11 (April 1935): 8

Conference to be held at St. Olaf's Lutheran Church. Several other articles in the *Star Tribune* note that Gruhn preached, spoke, and organized events or programs during the two years he served at Wesley Methodist Church. One picture shows Gruhn at the door of the church, greeting Aunt Dot and other young people. A final article on June 12, 1937, says that he had resigned to accept a similar post at a Lutheran church in Des Moines, and the Methodist congregation would be giving him a farewell reception.

During their three years in Minneapolis, Gruhn had the daily rigors of classes and study, as well as the goal of earning his B.D. and S.T.M. degrees. Aunt Dot would have had only the daily grind of work, which may or may not have been challenging. She had no network of family, friends, or church connections when she moved to Minneapolis. Her only long-term challenge or goal would have been to earn money and prepare for setting up housekeeping, since she was not contemplating a career in business. Her weekly short-term goal may have simply been to look forward to her next date with Gruhn. He would undoubtedly have talked about his studies and daily activities, so she may have lived vicariously through him. It seems unlikely that she would have enjoyed any intellectual stimulation except through his talking about his studies or perhaps in listening to a Sunday sermon. Other than living in a large urban setting, Aunt Dot's life would have been substantially contracted from her college years. She must have been banking everything on her dream of a future, happy marriage, and home.

Given their respective ethnic and religious backgrounds, such a dream was not out of the question. Similar to Aunt Dot's own father, August Gruhn Sr., had emigrated from Prussia as a boy of 6 and settled with family in Canada. He worked in factories at the age of 9 and then became an apprentice tailor. But his heart was, apparently, in the work of the church. He was encouraged to prepare for the ministry. To that end, when in his early 30s, he moved to Buffalo, New York, and entered seminary. After graduation, he was ordained in 1902 and served several parishes in Canada and this country before being called as a hospital chaplain and then to the pulpit of Redeemer Lutheran Church in Milwaukee. That church belonged to the English Evangelical Synod of the Northwest, and Northwestern Lutheran Seminary was its training school for future ministers.[21] August Gruhn Sr. married a young woman in Canada, and that accounts for the fact that August Jr. was born in Canada. The family moved to this country when he was only a baby.

---

[21] "Deceased: Rev. August Gruhn," *The Lutheran* (January 13, 1954): 46.

Thus, Gruhn came from a synod that emphasized the English language, unlike other theological bodies that tended to emphasize their German background. In a similar pattern, Grandpa Wagner, though a businessman, had been strongly influenced by Rev. Blancke at St. Paul English Evangelical Lutheran Church in Davenport. Thus, Gruhn and Aunt Dot both came from a German Lutheran family background but with an English language emphasis, as well as attending the same Lutheran college. They would both have been imbued with common core values. Although Rev. Blancke was no longer at St. Paul when she was confirmed, Aunt Dot would have learned the traditional Lutheran catechism and been taught the importance of marriage and family as then held by the ULCA. Their statement on the family, printed in the Minutes of their Biennial Convention in 1928, affirmed:

> That the family is a divine institution and that the orderly governance of the life of mankind is directly dependent upon the preservation of its integrity and stability.[22]

In 1930, the same convention stated its conviction about the importance of marriage:

> The United Lutheran Church, in accordance with the teaching of the Scriptures, holds that marriage is a holy estate, ordained of God, and to be held in honor by all. It deeply deplores the increasing disregard of the sanctity of the marriage tie, and solemnly protests against all teaching and practice which violates this sanctity and are therefore contrary to the revealed will of God.[23]

As a seminarian, Gruhn would have been thoroughly instructed in the church's teaching about marriage and family. Maybe he even lectured Aunt Dot on the church's belief. Given their family and faith backgrounds, it must have seemed to Aunt Dot that marriage to this future Lutheran minister was an ideal choice for her. His credentials suggested she was waiting to marry a winner.

In a biographical sketch that Gruhn wrote in February 1942, he listed his education and church work prior to his seminary training. In 1926, he had been elected President of the Milwaukee District Luther League.

---

[22] II. Religion and the Family, 1928: Minutes, 6th Biennial Convention, ULCA, in *Social Statements of the United Lutheran Church in America 1918-1962*, foreword Rufus Cornelsen (New York: Board of Social Missions of the ULCA, 1962), 80.

[23] III. Marriage, Family and Divorce, 1930: Minutes, 7th Biennial Convention, ULCA (Loc. Cit.), 81.

Then, in 1928, he became the Wisconsin State Luther League President for two years. Having graduated from Concordia Academy and Junior College in Milwaukee in 1929, he served as a parish worker at Hollywood Lutheran Church in California during 1930. Following that term of service, he enrolled at Carthage College and was graduated in 1933, whereupon he immediately entered Northwestern Lutheran Seminary.

Gruhn received his B.D. degree in 1936 and the S.T.M. graduate degree in 1937. Upon receiving a call to St. John's Lutheran Church in Des Moines, he was ordained in his father's church in Milwaukee, Redeemer Lutheran, on June 10, 1937. He began his pastoral work in Des Moines on June 15, specializing in "the work of evangelism, men's and youth organizations."

We have no way of finding out if Aunt Dot was invited to his ordination ceremony in Milwaukee and to meet his family. We have no way of knowing if Grandpa and Grandma Wagner ever met August Gruhn before Aunt Dot married him. We do not know how long Aunt Dot remained in Minneapolis. There are no records that can be traced and no known family members that could be asked. When next we find Aunt Dot, she is to be married in St. John's Lutheran Church in Des Moines.

Notes

- Regarding distances and city transportation, I relied on my own recollections of riding the streetcars in Minneapolis when I was a child, as well as seeing the original Sears store when shopping with my aunt in the mid-town area in the 1940s. Driving to see the building that had housed the Northwestern Seminary during Gruhn's years there helped me to understand distances he and Aunt Dot would have had to plan into their commutes in order to see each other.
- With no family knowledge of when and where Aunt Dot and Gruhn were married, I contacted a researcher in the Des Moines area and asked her to check the Iowa department of vital records to search for a marriage certificate. Her work led me to the Davenport newspaper which announced their forthcoming marriage.

THE DAILY TIMES, FRIDAY, DECEMBER 24, 1937

Wagner-Gruhn Wedding to Follow Midnight Service

FOLLOWING the midnight services tonight in St. John's Lutheran church, Des Moines, with many candles casting a soft glow on the Christmas decorations, Miss Dorothy Louise Wagner, daughter of Mr. and Mrs C. H. Wagner of 2925 Brady street, Davenport, will become the bride of the assistant pastor, the Rev. August W. Gruhn, son of the Rev. and Mrs A. Gruhn of Milwaukee, Wis.

The choir will sing a nuptial song after which the organist will play the familiar "Bridal Chorus" from 'Lohengrin" as the bridal party take their places before the altar.

Miss Viola Mathowetz of Minneapolis will attend as maid of honor and Mr Karl Gruhn of Minneapolis will serve his brother as best man.

The bride will wear a white crepe gown embroidered in silver and a silver lame jacket with long sleeves. A finger tip length veil will be held at the coiffure with a silver lame cap. She will carry gardenias. Miss Mathowetz will be in a dark green moire gown and her flowers will be violets.

The bridal couple will come to Davenport to have Christmas dinner with the bride's parents. They will leave later for Milwaukee and northern Wisconsin, and will be at home in Des Moines by Jan. 7.

The bride is a graduate of the Davenport high school and attended Carthage college in Carthage, Ill., of which Rev. Gruhn is an alumnus. He later was graduated from the Northwestern Lutheran Theological seminary in Minneapolis and was ordained to the ministry last June in Milwaukee. He has since been the assistant pastor at St. John's Lutheran church in Des Moines.

MISS DOROTHY WAGNER

CHAPTER FOUR

A Wedding with Clouds in View

Both the *Davenport Democrat and Leader,* as well as the *Daily Times,* carried Aunt Dot's picture, which shows her without glasses and wearing a short, softly curled hair style common in the 1930s. According to the *Times* for Friday, December 24, 1937:

> Following the midnight services tonight in St. John's Lutheran church, Des Moines, with many candles casting a soft glow on the Christmas decorations, Miss Dorothy Louise Wagner, daughter of Mr. and Mrs. C. H. Wagner of 2925 Brady Street, Davenport, will become the bride of the assistant pastor, the Rev. August W. Gruhn, son of the Rev. and Mrs. A. Gruhn of Milwaukee, Wis.

The church choir was to sing, and the church organist would play "the familiar 'Bridal Chorus' from 'Lohengrin' as the bridal party take their places" in front of the altar. Miss Viola Mathiowetz of Minneapolis was to attend Aunt Dot as maid of honor. Karl Gruhn, brother of the groom, would serve as best man.

The description of Aunt Dot's dress sounds elegant. She was to wear "a white crepe gown embroidered in silver and a silver lamé jacket with long sleeves. A finger-tip length veil will be held at the coiffure with a silver lamé cap. She will carry gardenias." The bridesmaid would wear "a dark green moire gown" and carry violets. With Aunt Dot's tall, slender figure and thick black hair framed against a silver cap and shining dress, she must have looked both regal and radiant amid the soft glow of candles.

According to the article in the *Times,* the newlyweds would drive to Davenport and have Christmas dinner with the bride's parents. They would "leave later for Milwaukee and northern Wisconsin, and be at home in Des Moines by January 7." The stop in Milwaukee would have been to see the groom's parents.

While the initial reading of this announcement sounded romantic, I could not help but realize that there was nothing traditional about the whole affair. The wedding was at the groom's church not, as custom dictated, at the bride's church. No families were present. Karl Gruhn was probably the only family member from either side to be in attendance. The whole arrangement suggested to me that the timing was Gruhn's choice. It certainly made him center stage in this church where he was the new assistant pastor. I wondered again about the degree to which Aunt Dot had acquiesced to Gruhn's ideas. Her wedding dress sounded elegant, but she probably wore it for little more than an hour, since a reception at 1:00 a.m. sounded unlikely. Who would stay for a reception following a midnight wedding on Christmas Eve? The modern reader could logically conclude that Gruhn chose to make Aunt Dot his trophy bride in front of a full sanctuary. The senior pastor, Rev. F. J. Weertz, performed the ceremony, and he had made St. John's a very big Lutheran church.

After considering the non-traditional arrangement of this wedding, I could not help but wonder what Grandpa and Grandma had thought about this marriage of their only daughter. They themselves had been married in the Stoltenberg home in northwest Davenport, the home in which Grandma had grown up, at a time when in-home weddings were common in Davenport. They had not been to Hardt's wedding on Christmas Eve in 1925 in South Bend, Indiana, very probably because Grandpa worked, and Christmas was a very busy season in retail. Grandpa and Grandma could not have afforded the cost in time and money to travel by train from Davenport to South Bend and then stay in a hotel. But when Hardt married Helen McCorkle, it was at the home church of her grandparents and was in the early evening of Christmas Eve. When Hub married Olive Torgeson in the small town of Beresford, South Dakota, Hardt and Helen drove Grandpa, Grandma, and Gene to that wedding, held at the home of the bride's mother. When Gene married Caroline Van Meter at the Van Meter family church across the river from Davenport, in Moline, Illinois, the whole family attended the wedding. We can only wonder if Grandpa and Grandma did not feel terribly slighted at Aunt Dot's wedding ceremony taking place away from their own home church in Davenport and at a time when they could not attend, given the reality that Grandpa was still working in retail.

When reading the newspaper description of Aunt Dot's wedding, I also wondered who Viola Mathiowetz was. That sent me back to the Minneapolis *City Directory* once I had verified that she was not in Aunt Dot's high school class. I found a Viola Mathiowetz in the Minneapolis *City Directory*, living in north Minneapolis in the mid-1930s when Aunt Dot moved to the city. I initially concluded that the two young women met at work or, perhaps, at the beauty shop, which the *City Directory* said was run by Viola's mother, Alvina Mathiowetz. However, the 1937 *Directory* says that Viola was an assistant at the Lyons Studio. Further research indicated that was a dance studio. Aunt Dot had taken a year of tap dancing at Carthage College. Perhaps the two women met at the studio. Regardless of where and how Aunt Dot met Viola, they certainly became good friends for Viola to travel to Des Moines to attend Aunt Dot as maid of honor.

We have no way of knowing when Aunt Dot quit her job in Minneapolis and whether or not she traveled to Davenport first for a short time or went directly to Des Moines. It is certainly a reasonable assumption that she might have gone home to Davenport for a couple of months to make her own wedding dress and have Grandma help her. Viola might then have visited in Davenport for a week before the wedding. She and Aunt Dot could easily have taken a bus to Des Moines. Whether or not Aunt Dot kept in contact with Viola after the wedding, we have no way of knowing. In the absence of any family recollections passed down to us cousins or kept in a diary, we will never know the full details about this short chapter in Aunt Dot's life.

It was much easier to locate Karl Gruhn, who served his brother as best man. In a family of six brothers, August was second oldest and Karl the next born. He was about two years younger than August and the only one of the surviving brothers who did not finish college and go on to seminary or graduate school. In 1937, according to the Minneapolis *City Directory*, Karl Gruhn was working at the Real Silk Hosiery Mills, probably as a salesman. Being single and living in Minneapolis where Gruhn had been studying, it is not surprising that Karl served as best man.

The newspaper article of the wedding reported that the newlyweds would be at home in Des Moines on January 7, 1938. That was the day Aunt Dot was taken into membership at St. John's Lutheran Church, according to her membership record provided by the church archive. It was a large congregation belonging to the ULCA but locally to the Iowa Synod. Aunt Dot would have felt right at home, given that she had grown up in St. Paul Lutheran in Davenport, also a member of the Iowa Synod.

Searching the Des Moines *City Directory* for where the newlyweds lived during their time in Des Moines raised a number of questions pointing to non-traditional arrangements. Gruhn's pastoral roll sheet for 1937, dated December 20, indicates that he lived at 715 Hickman Road.

As early as December 5, the Des Moines newspaper article announcing his forthcoming marriage also said he resided at the same address. We do not know if Gruhn selected this residence by himself or in consultation with Aunt Dot.

The street address of 715 Hickman Road identified a very large home built in 1905 and located in a section of Des Moines known as the Prospect Park Second Plat Historic District on the National Register of Historic Places. The house was named the Benjamin A. Lockwood House after the local capitalist who lived in it during his career. Although the house was converted into apartments in 1954, the 1938 *City Directory* lists only the Gruhns and a Leonard F. Blair and wife as renters. If the entire house had been converted into only two apartments of about equal size, each family had ample space; total square footage amounted to 7,428.

Several factors made this home a non-traditional one for a new associate pastor and his wife. First, although we do not know the amount of their rent or the exact space available to them, it may have been more than they needed as a newly married couple. Neither Aunt Dot nor Gruhn would have come from inherited wealth. Although he had been receiving a small salary as assistant at Wesley Methodist Church in Minneapolis and Aunt Dot had also been working at Sears Roebuck, it is unlikely that they would have been able to accumulate a large savings account. The economy was still just plugging along in the later-1930s. Moreover, the Gruhns had to buy furniture, dishes, linens, etc., in order to furnish an apartment.

Second, 715 Hickman Road was located about two miles from St. John's Lutheran Church, according to a city map of the time. The senior pastor lived in a house provided by the church, as was typical of the era. Arthur Simonsen, the other associate pastor, and his wife lived in the same apartment near the church from 1938 through 1941, according to the *City Directory*. A local map of the era suggests that Simonsen had an easy walk to the church from their apartment. According to the ELCA archive, there are no records indicating whether or not the church supplied housing for associate pastors or gave them money for housing. It seems curious that Gruhn chose to live so much farther from the church than did Simonsen. It was definitely not in Aunt Dot's background to aspire to such a large, expensive-looking house and/or to live beyond one's means.

The third unusual factor about where the Gruhns lived is the reality that they moved at least four times between January 1938 and spring of

1942. According to the *City Directory* for 1939, they had moved out of the house at 715 Hickman Road and into an apartment at 1802 Oakland Avenue. However, Aunt Dot's membership record at the church says that her address was 1802 Oakland in 1938. No month is written in to indicate when the move occurred. If the data for the 1939 *City Directory* had been gathered in late December or early January, the Gruhns might have moved months earlier in 1938. Not far from the Hickman Road address, this apartment building was also in the historic district of the city called "The Oaklands."

Also unusual for the era, Aunt Dot is listed twice in the 1939 *City Directory*, once as Dorothea L., wife of Rev. August W. Gruhn, and a second time as Dorothy W, stenographer for the Iowa Retail Sales Tax Division. Both listings for her cite the 1802 Oakland residence. The Des Moines Building, where her job was located, stood not far from the church. That would have been about two miles for her to get to work. However, there were well-established streetcar lines to ride if Gruhn decided that he had to drive a car to the church. Certainly, his hours on the job could have been very irregular, compared to Aunt Dot's.

For the wife of a minister to be working outside the home in that era suggests that the Gruhns may have been in financial straits. Aunt Dot had worked as a stenographer in Davenport at the Hospital Supply Company and also in Minneapolis at Sears Roebuck for one year. Thus, she had at least two years experience when she applied at the Iowa Retail Sales Tax Division. We do not know if that division was part of the federal bureaucracy, but a report published in 1941 sheds some light on salaries for a job like Aunt Dot held. According to a 1938 survey of women in the federal government, senior stenographers had to be competent at the rate of 120 words per minute and commanded a salary of $1,620. Junior stenographers received that classification if they were competent at the rate of ninety-six words per minute. They usually earned somewhere between $1,400 and $1,200 annually.[24] Even though Aunt Dot's salary in Des Moines might have been much less, still her paycheck could have made a significant difference to their household income for 1939. Had she made $1,000 for the year, it would have been about half of Gruhn's salary for the year 1940.

Yet another change or changes in their residence occurred in that year. The Gruhns are listed in the 1940 *City Directory* as still residing at

---

[24] Rachel Fesler Nyswander and Janet M. Hooks, *Employment of Women in the Federal Government 1923-1939* (Washington: U.S. Dept. of Labor, Government Printing Office, 1941), 21.

1802 Oakland. However, Aunt Dot's church membership card says she lived at 1820 Oakland as of January 1940. The telephone book for 1940 also lists 1820 Oakland. When the U.S. census was taken in early April, their address was 410 Franklin. That house, like their first residence, was built in 1905, listed in "The Oaklands" Historic District and known as the George H. France House, an example of the Prairie School of architecture. The census also reports that the Gruhns paid $55 a month for rent, and he earned an annual salary of $2,100. Though not as spacious as the house on Hickman Road, the Franklin Avenue home was still ample—4,504 square feet. However, the census also indicates that the house had been broken up into six apartments. The rents paid, listed in order of entry on the census form were $80, $58, $55, $65, $60, and $30 per month. So the Gruhns apparently had space and amenities that fell into the lower half of the rental range.

Puzzling data from the *City Directory* further complicates our understanding of their living situation. At the back of the *Directory* for 1939, 1940, and 1941, residents are listed by street address. That listing gives an Arabic number after the name of, presumably, the head of the household. According to the Des Moines Public Library, that numeral referred to the number of persons living at the address. For the three years cited, the *City Directory* printed the number three after Gruhn's name. For a third person to be living with the young marrieds seems unusual. However, the 1940 census cites only Gruhn and Aunt Dot at the 410 Franklin residence. Specific instructions on the census form said to name every person who resided at the address on a temporary or permanent basis, and Aunt Dot is denoted as the one who provided the information for the census taker.

Further confusing the evidence is the lack of clarity about the time of year when the Des Moines *City Directory* was published each year. The public library staff could not definitively identify the month of publication, but they estimated February. Adding to the mystery is the fact that address changes on Aunt Dot's church membership record lacked day or month. Moreover, the address of 410 Franklin, given on their census form, is not recorded at all on her membership card. The church would not give out any addresses for Rev. Gruhn.

The 1942 *City Directory* finds the Gruhns residing at 253 Franklin Avenue, an address not listed in Aunt Dot's church membership record. That document has her living at 810 Hickman Road for 1941. Gruhn's records from the ELCA archive include two telegrams sent and received by him in February 1942. His address on both telegrams is 810 Hickman

Road. This one-and-a-half story house, built in 1917, was still in the Historic District and probably a single family dwelling.

Despite the several mysteries surrounding their residences, it seems safe to say that the Gruhns moved at least four, and perhaps five times, during their stay in Des Moines of four-and-a-half years. The contrast with Arthur Simonsen, the other associate pastor, and his wife is dramatic. They remained in the same apartment near the church from 1938 through 1941, even when a baby daughter entered their household in 1940. Since the church would have needed to know addresses and phone numbers of its pastors on an annual basis, it seems probable that Gruhn would have had some ready answers for the senior pastor, Weertz, and the other assistant, Simonsen. They would surely have asked why the Gruhns moved annually. They may also have wondered why Aunt Dot worked outside the home in 1939.

Regardless of how Gruhn explained their annual changes of residence, we can safely assume that the burden of packing, cleaning, moving, and furnishing yet another home always fell to Aunt Dot. That was the wife's role which Gruhn would have known from his mother's work during his growing up years. Aunt Dot knew the same role from her mother. Whether or not Aunt Dot liked this role of housekeeper, with no outside income, we have no way of knowing. But, it was a common role for women of that era, especially as typified by the label "housewife." However, the wife of a minister also had special responsibilities or, at least, expectations laid upon her by the congregation in which her husband served.

The usual role for a pastor's wife in that era was to participate in the ladies aid, the missionary society, the altar guild, perhaps to teach a Sunday school class and/or to sing in the choir. Women would not have served on the church council or a building committee or managed any financial operations. Of course, pastors' wives also took care of their children. But Aunt Dot had no children. My cousin Nancy, daughter of Aunt Dot's brother, Gene, remembers her father telling her that Aunt Dot could not have children. But Nancy was very young when she asked her father why Aunt Dot had no children of her own, and he didn't give Nancy any specific anatomical or physiological details. Nancy's recollections about her father's medical career, plus the 1940 census and Des Moines *City Directory*, tell us that Aunt Dot's brother was living and working nearby beginning in 1940.

Gene had saved enough money from his three years of teaching, following graduation from Carthage College, that he could enroll in the

University of Iowa Medical School in the summer of 1934. Graduating in 1938, he went east for his internship at St. John Hospital in Younkers, New York. Whether he interned for over a year or completed six months of residency there, Nancy does not know for sure. But the 1940 Census, taken April 2, finds him listed as the only resident physician at Methodist Hospital in Des Moines. There is one resident surgeon who is paid $1,200. Dr. E. C. Wagner is reported as making $600. However, we do not know when that pay started. Gene and the surgeon each worked fifty-two weeks, according to the census.

Despite working long hours for little pay, Gene managed to keep up his long distance courtship with Caroline Van Meter, who worked in Cedar Rapids, Iowa. She had to take a bus to Des Moines to see him, and they had no private time or space together. But they had written and dated during Gene's residency in Yonkers, New York, so their relationship was tested over many months. They married in October 1940. Gene asked Gruhn to be his best man. This selection seemed to Nancy and me a bit odd, but perhaps Gene did not want family brothers to be jealous of one selected over the other. Hardt, Hub, and Caroline's brother, Herb Van Meter, all served as ushers at the wedding in the Congregational church in Moline where the family had been long-time members.

Gene's selection of Gruhn to serve as best man suggests that the two had known each other for a while. Gene probably attended St. John's Lutheran Church when his medical duties permitted. Certainly, Gene had been close to Aunt Dot during their growing up years; he was not quite four years older than she. When Hub went off to Carthage College in the fall of 1921, Gene was just over 12 years; Aunt Dot was only 8½. From those early years, they were the two siblings at home together during the school months of each year until Gene went off to college. His kind personality would have made him sensitive to and protective of Aunt Dot as a young girl. Whether he thought she should have quit college or not, he would have been concerned for her well-being. When she did not become pregnant, he might have referred her to an ob-gyn colleague in Des Moines.

Once Gene and Caroline were married, they returned to Des Moines to live. By this time, Gene was earning a salary as Assistant Director of the Iowa Department of Public Health division of preventable diseases and epidemiology. Nancy remembers her mother saying that she and Gene lived in a large, old home that had been made into apartments. Telephone books for 1941 and 1942 list the Wagners at 253 Franklin. In addition, Gene's World War II bonus case file confirms that he resided at 253 Franklin for the six months prior to his induction into the army. What is puzzling is that the *City Directory* for 1941 lists only Gene, and he is at the same address it lists for the Gruhns—1820 Oakland, Apt. 6. If the data for that *Directory* were gathered in 1940, before Gene and Caroline were married in late October, Gene may have lived with the Gruhns for a short time before his marriage and after he quit as resident physician at Methodist Hospital. If so, that could account for the number three after Gruhn's name in the *City Directory*. It could also account for Gene asking Gruhn to be his best man.

Nancy has no recollection of her mother telling about moving to another apartment during their approximately one-and-a-half years in Des Moines. She did, however, hear interesting anecdotes about the somewhat eccentric woman who owned the mansion that had been made into apartments. So it seems safe to assume that the Wagners resided at 253 Franklin for their entire stay in Des Moines. This meant they lived near the Gruhns; the sisters-in-law may have spent a good deal of time together as neither of them had children.

We will never know directly how Aunt Dot spent her days as a housewife. We can only estimate her daily activity based on women's roles in the homes of the early 1940s. First, she would have had to prepare meals from scratch. Frozen foods, cake mixes, dehydrated casseroles, etc., did not exist. Following Grandma's role model, Aunt Dot would probably have baked bread, rolls, coffee cakes, and pies. Since her refrigerator either had no freezer at all or, at best, only a tiny capacity beneath the ice cube trays, she would have had to go to the grocery store and meat market several times weekly. Large supermarkets with everything under one roof also did not exist in that era. If those stores were not close by, she had to walk or ride a streetcar; the Gruhns would not have owned two cars. Second, in addition to food preparation, Aunt Dot would have managed weekly laundry, ironing, and mending. Washing clothes could have been very time-consuming in an apartment, assuming a central laundry operation and many flights of stairs. Clothes had to be hung on a line to dry. Automatic washers and dryers were a long ways into the future. Further, if she did not have a sewing machine, any sewing of clothes, curtains, tablecloths, etc., had to be done by hand. All in all, Aunt Dot would have been very busy on a daily basis just keeping their home clean and attractive and both of them well fed and clothed. How she managed their annual moves to a new abode is a wonder. Moreover, how she managed to work at the Iowa Retail Sales Tax Division during 1939 is almost incomprehensible. We can only imagine that she was chronically fatigued.

We do know, though, that she had some friends. Newspaper articles from those years report that she had been a bridal attendant in two weddings. She must have made friends easily, as her friendship with Viola Mathiowetz in Minneapolis suggested. But again, absent any diaries, letters, or direct family recollections, we have another void in trying to reconstruct Aunt Dot's married life. We can, however, learn a great deal about Gruhn, his associates and their work in the church. By inference, we can draw some additional insights about the kind of life Aunt Dot experienced in those years just prior to World War II.

When August Gruhn came to St. John's Lutheran as an associate pastor in June 1937, he joined another young man who was also coming in June. Arthur M. Simonsen was two years older than Gruhn, according to church documents and census data, but the two young clergymen shared many of the same characteristics. They were both in their late 20s; both were married; and neither had children as of 1937. Both grew up in the Midwest, with fathers as ministers. Both had gone to Lutheran colleges as well as seminaries in the Midwest. Simonsen brought two years of experience as the pastor of two Lutheran churches in small Iowa towns. By contrast, Gruhn had spent his first two years of seminary as a student assistant at a large and affluent Lutheran church in north Minneapolis. St. Olaf Lutheran Church, for example, had built a sanctuary in 1911 that seated 500 persons. And their minister in 1933, according to the church yearbook, was paid a salary of $2,900. In Gruhn's last two years of seminary, he served as a youth pastor at a large Methodist church in downtown Minneapolis. Thus, he brought a more cosmopolitan background than did Simonsen and had been more involved in evangelism and youth work.

When Gruhn and Simonsen went to St. John's, they were to serve under Rev. Frederick J. Weertz, who was about twenty years older than the young assistants. Weertz had held the pulpit since 1925 and was particularly interested in evangelism. Unlike the young assistants, Weertz had come to faith and the ministry after a youth spent running away from home and trying varied activities. His father had been a butcher in Chicago. Weertz did not like that business and left home at age 11. Eventually the youth found some success in the boxing ring. It was after a tough fight in Albuquerque that he determined to quit the boxing ring and turn his life over to God. Thus, Weertz was older than the normal youth when he attended Midland Lutheran College as well as Western Seminary in Fremont, Nebraska. Just out of seminary and before coming to Des Moines, Weertz served four years as an assistant pastor in a large Lutheran church in Omaha.

With this background, it is understandable that Weertz was particularly interested in evangelism. When he came to St. John's in 1925, the church counted only 500 members. After being there only five years, he persuaded the church council to bring in an assistant, who served with Weertz from 1930 to 1937. Very likely the senior pastor's sermons were what drew people to the church. An article in the *Des Moines Tribune* on April 28, 1956, recapping his career, makes clear that he was no ordinary preacher:

> Dr. Weertz is as much a fighting man in the pulpit as he ever was in the ring. Gifted with a full resonant voice, a sense of the dramatic, the magnetism of a cracker barrel storyteller, he pounds and gestures, roars and whispers to put across his sermon.

Presumably, then, when Gruhn and Simonsen were hired in June 1937, the size of the congregation and the duties of the pastors required two assistants instead of one. Looking at this troika heading up a growing metropolitan church suggests that difficulty would lie ahead. Seminary curricula of that day tended to emphasize theology and pastoral duties, as well as preaching, but not necessarily administrative or human relations skills and strategy. Gruhn may have had far more experience than Simonsen in dealing with a senior pastor. However, pastors' individual personalities also entered into the dynamics of preaching, organizing, evangelizing, and ministering.

A look at Gruhn's family background and birth order suggests that he was probably a very competitive and dominant individual. August W. Gruhn was named after his father. Like Weertz, the senior Gruhn had worked in trades from a very young age. So he, like Weertz, attended college and seminary at a later age than the normal matriculation to college at age 18. Thus, married late, August Gruhn Sr. and his wife raised a family of ten children. August W. Gruhn was the third oldest child, but the second oldest son. He followed his older brother, Harold, who eventually became pastor at the church their father had served in Milwaukee. The younger brother, Victor, also attended college and seminary and eventually became a pastor at a very large church in the Chicago area. Karl, who served August as best man, was between August and Victor. The two youngest brothers, born after Victor, both served in World War II. Given this synopsis of Gruhn's family, as well as his own background, it seems probable that he came to St. John's Lutheran in Des Moines with considerable energy and ambition to make a name and mark for himself.

How Gruhn and Aunt Dot related to each other is another story. Given the ideal for women at that time, Aunt Dot surely entered her marriage with every expectation that she had made a wonderful choice and that their marriage would last a lifetime, as she had experienced in her own home in Davenport. She would have brought domestic skills, money management skills, and the intellectual background that two years of college had provided, plus a confidence in her own ability to perform well in jobs that her experience in Davenport and Minneapolis had provided. Moreover, she would have expected to be able to speak her mind and be listened to, based on her home background with three older and well-educated brothers. She would not have expected to be a doormat for her husband.

By contrast, Gruhn had grown up with a mother over twenty years younger than her husband. According to census data, she was about 18 when married. She bore ten children over twenty-one years. That would have left her little time for anything other than bearing and rearing children, cooking, washing, and cleaning house. It seems a truism that most people bring their own home and family background to their marriages and future expectations. Given their different family experiences, it seems very likely that Gruhn and Aunt Dot held expectations and points of view that would inevitably clash. Nothing in Gruhn's known personality and background suggests that he would have been open to negotiating differences with Aunt Dot. Given the widely held view of the importance of clergy in that era and the strong male dominance in Gruhn's home when he grew up, it seems likely that he would have expected Aunt Dot to agree with him when differences of opinion became obvious. Since it was extremely unusual in that era for young people to live together before marriage, the Gruhns would have encountered a multiplicity of areas that required discussion and negotiation once they were married, not the least of which would have been money and budgets.

In addition, Gruhn would very likely have encountered a number of areas at the church in which he, Weertz, and Simonsen did not always see eye to eye. Weertz was, by all accounts, a strong personality. He had had only one assistant prior to the arrival of Gruhn and Simonsen. Weertz may or may not have acquired any administrative skills, and he may not have thought through carefully just how to make the best use of these new young men. In addition, Weertz was suffering from health problems and had been advised to move to California in the hope that the climate would prove palliative. In fact, he did move to a church in Los Angeles in the fall of 1940, but came back the following summer or fall. So he was absent from Des Moines for a year, perhaps less. Weertz's presence and absence would surely have added a challenging element to an already potentially lethal mix. Personalities, division of authority, and degrees of supervision would have triggered rivalry. In this situation, the seriousness of conflict escalated over time until it finally burst forth on the front page of the *Des Moines Tribune* in January 1942. Two articles in the paper that month give background and resolution.

The opening paragraph of the story printed on January 16 tells the core issue:

> In one of the most spirited meetings of its history, St. John's Evangelical Lutheran Church Thursday night heard its two assistant pastors offer their resignations during an open discussion of lack of harmony among the church's three pastors.

Continuing the description of the meeting, the reporter called it a "tense discussion" that took place over three hours, amid "cheers and boos" as different members of the congregation came to the microphone to express their opinions. Each of the three pastors was invited to state his case. When Gruhn spoke, he pleaded for the conflict not to be decided by the congregation. "It will tear us asunder." He also firmly asserted that he had "never been insubordinate." When Simonsen took the microphone, he said Weertz had claimed that the congregation was "facing chaos" if he did not return. When Weertz himself talked, he claimed that the assistant pastors felt they had done good work in the past and had not received credit for it. In effect, the story suggests that each pastor presented what he thought was true, but in the process justified his own actions. The final break came eleven days later.

On January 27, the *Des Moines Tribune* printed the story on its front page. The column headline read: "2 Resign Posts at St. John's." Gruhn and Simonsen had submitted their resignations to the church council the night before. The council had accepted their resignations and voted each man an honorarium of $400 in recognition of the "splendid service" rendered by them over the past four-and-a-half years. This announcement came from Alex Miller, attorney and member of the church council. Gruhn and Simonsen were to end their duties at the church immediately but would remain on the payroll until February 15 when their salaries would cease and the honoraria would be added to their final pay.

Additional paragraphs explained the probable cause of friction among the pastors. The three had worked together from their advent at St. John's until November 1940, a time of about three-and-a-half years. Then Weertz went to a church in Los Angeles to try and regain his health. However, in June 1941, factions in St. John's urged him to return. Attorney Miller explained that, in Weertz' absence, Gruhn and Simonsen each carried out separate domains of responsibility and reported directly to the church council. Each had been given a free hand by the council. When Weertz returned, both assistants were again directly responsible to the senior pastor, and therein lay the source of controversy. No longer did the assistants have a free hand in determining how they were going to go about their duties. Interestingly, the article closes by stating that St. John's had a membership of "more than 3,000," and was the second largest Lutheran church in the country. Reportedly, the largest was North Austin Lutheran in Chicago, where Gruhn's younger brother, Victor, was a pastor.

With all of this congregational friction finally out in the open, it seems obvious that opinions had been roiling for months. For some to write Weertz in June 1941 and ask him to return, clearly factions had been formed at least by that time. Tensions would have grown upon his return in the fall. We can only wonder at how Gruhn handled tension, criticism, and opposition. What did he bring home? How much did he discuss with Aunt Dot? To what degree did she offer her opinions? How did he respond?

At this point in the story, we are faced with oral history based on long-ago memories held by my cousins and me. At some point when I had begun researching the Wagner family history, I recalled a fragment from the dim past. I remembered nothing other than a statement from my father that he had gone down to the bus depot in Davenport to pick up Aunt Dot and she had a black eye. I do not know how old I was at this time, and I do not recall asking him anything more. I think I was probably not more than 12 or 13, maybe younger. However, I retained the distinct impression that the black eye did not come from walking into a door.

When writing our family history, I had many conversations with cousin Nancy, because she was the acknowledged "family historian" for Gene's family. In one conversation, Nancy told about a recollection of hers regarding what we called the "black eye incident." Long after Aunt Dot had married John Zambon, her second husband, Nancy remembered asking her mother, Caroline, if Aunt Dot had been married before. Caroline responded yes, but her first husband had "not been nice to Aunt Dot." In fact, he was a "hypocrite." Nancy said she recalled this conversation specifically because she, at age 8, knew what the word hypocrite meant.

On another occasion in the 1950s, Nancy's younger sister, Kate, also queried her mother about this second husband. When Aunt Dot and Uncle John came north each summer for their vacation, they visited Gene's family at their home in Plainfield, Iowa, where Gene was practicing as a small town and country doctor. In one telephone conversation with me, Kate remembered asking her mother what she thought of Uncle John. Kate said her mother responded, "It doesn't matter what I think of him; he is kind to Aunt Dot." Neither Nancy nor Kate had been in communication about Aunt Dot and her marriages for decades. And neither had ever before talked with me about this issue.

Further perspective came to me from Ginny Wagner, widow of my cousin Les, who was the son of Aunt Dot's oldest brother, Hardt. Ginny has lived for decades in northwest Washington state. I spoke with her regularly after Les died in order to get as many family history details as I could from that branch of the Wagner family. In one such conversation, Ginny said that when she and Les were young married folk, in the early 1960s, they often sat around the kitchen table at Hardt's home in Dallas and heard anecdotes and stories of family history. Ginny recalled clear impressions rather than specific statements. She said that she had the distinct impression that Aunt Dot suffered abuse at the hand of August Gruhn and that "bruises did appear." She also recalled that Hardt thought Aunt Dot should get out of the marriage, but that Grandma Wagner thought she should stay in the marriage. Ginny added further that Hardt did not normally talk about other people; she had the strong impression that Hardt cared very much about Aunt Dot.

Finally, when I began thinking and writing about Aunt Dot's first marriage, a recollection popped into my mind one day about a conversation I had had with my mother when I was in my early twenties. At that time, in the late 1950s, there was so much emphasis in our culture on women getting married that I was feeling as though I was a failure since I had just graduated from college but did not have a diamond on the third finger of my left hand. Whatever else my mother said has evaporated from my memory. But I well remember her saying rather adamantly, "Listen, there are worse things than not being married—like being married to the wrong man." At the time, I did not know anything at all about Aunt Dot's first marriage.

Clearly, there are pitfalls with using recollections to establish truth about a person's life. But the fact that we four cousins all retained fragments of memories from so may decades earlier and the fact that we had never before talked about any of these memories to each other, argues strongly that there was truth in our collective memory bank.

In further telephone conversations with Nancy, she recalled her mother saying that one time Aunt Dot came to the Wagner family home on Brady Street in Davenport with a black eye. She also said the three brothers were all present and were furious at this attack on their sister. It was some type of family gathering, so everyone was present.

In trying to discern the time, it seemed to me that it was probably August or September 1941. Grandma and Grandpa would have celebrated their fortieth wedding anniversary that September. It would have been an occasion for the entire family to gather. Hardt and family were living in a Chicago suburb and could have easily driven to Davenport. Hub was teaching and coaching at Carthage College, so the gathering may have been at the end of August, as he would have been involved in football during September. Gene and Caroline probably drove from Des Moines and took extra days so they could visit Caroline's parents in Moline on the trip. The occasion could not have happened a year earlier, since Gene and Caroline were not married until October 1940. Moreover, Nancy was sure that her father would not have asked Gruhn to be his best man if he had known of any domestic abuse. And the gathering could not have happened in 1942 since the war had begun, and both Gruhn and Gene were in the army. Thus, Nancy and I calculated that this family gathering at which Caroline remembered seeing Aunt Dot with a black eye occurred at the same time that the congregational disharmony at St. John's was gathering steam.

It would have been almost impossible for Gruhn to avoid bringing home his frustrations, tensions, probably anger—very likely a host of strong emotions. It seems likely that Aunt Dot would have voiced her views on the situation. She was used to Grandma speaking her mind and being respected by Grandpa. Did Aunt Dot say something that provoked Gruhn to hit her? Had there been other situations in which he hit her or threatened? By the fall of 1941, they had been married about three months short of three years.

In the 1930s there was little attention paid to spousal abuse. Families and the church kept quiet about such behavior. If Aunt Dot had experienced any prior physical abuse, she would have had virtually no place to go. Women's shelters did not exist. Presumably Caroline knew something of how Gruhn treated Aunt Dot or she would not, years later, have called him a "hypocrite" when Nancy asked about Aunt Dot's first husband. But, it is likely that Aunt Dot felt she should stick it out with Gruhn. That is what a good Lutheran did. One did not break marriage vows. It is also possible that Gruhn had verbally beaten her into submission, i.e. into thinking that his opinion was always right and her opinion was always wrong. With Gene and Caroline living nearby in Des Moines, Aunt Dot had the example of how Gene always treated Caroline with respect and loving devotion. So she would have known there was another and better marriage pattern than the one she was in. Yet she would also have known that no one would believe her if she told about Gruhn's private behavior in their own house. In addition, when one is involved in a pattern of abuse, the situation usually does not get bad suddenly. Abuse can escalate from subtle verbal putdowns to outright verbal demeaning; from calm voices to shouting matches; from shaking a fist to throwing objects to hitting the woman. But until such abuse becomes regular and frequent, the victim may not recognize what is happening to her. In the case of Aunt Dot, she may well have been browbeaten without realizing it. She may have thought that, of course, the minister was right. It was a man's world in the church and in the Midwest. She may have tried ever harder to please him or, at the least, to do nothing that would unleash his anger.

Amid all of the church controversy and factions lined up behind the three church pastors, the United States was attacked by the Empire of Japan on December 7, 1941. Once Gruhn and Simonsen decided to resign their positions, they had final pay coming on February 15. They had to make plans for their futures. Simonsen chose to stay in the parish ministry—not surprising since he and his wife had a baby daughter in 1940. He finished out his career in another Lutheran church in Des Moines and held several positions of responsibility in the city and in the synod.

Gruhn, however, chose to apply for the army chaplaincy and began that process by early February, 1942.

Whether or not he asked Aunt Dot's opinion, we do not know. But the entire country mobilized immediately. Aunt Dot would have known that Gene had gone down to the recruiting station in Des Moines on December 8 and applied for the army medical corps. Thus, in Aunt Dot's mind, it would have been logical and natural to have her husband follow suit and apply for the chaplaincy corps.

Given Gruhn's prior activities and behavior, it seems logical that the army chaplaincy appealed to him far more than serving in the parish ministry. The whole country was patriotic and behind our armed forces. A man in uniform was looked up to. It seems likely that the image of a man of faith—a chaplain—who was in uniform held an appeal for Gruhn that could not be matched by merely serving as pastor of a single parish. A position in the army chaplaincy would have carried authority, order, travel to unknown theaters of war, and chances for promotion. He would not have had to do any fund-raising, or teach confirmation to thirteen year olds, or solve relationship problems with volunteers and/or with other churches and boards in the community. The army would have offered strict chain of command, regular pay, and the opportunity to have his sermons spread far beyond a local church. Amid a nation caught up in patriotism, the opportunity for glory, probably cloaked in his own mind as duty, would have been hard to resist.

Notes

- The reality that no family members attended the wedding can be inferred from the newspaper article. Typically, society pages of that era, when reporting on weddings, would tell what the mothers of the bride and groom wore or were going to wear and also identify out-of-town guests. They would also usually tell about a reception or wedding dinner. Since all such information is lacking in the *Daily Times* article, it seems reasonable to assume that no family members, other than the groom's brother, attended the wedding.
- The Des Moines Public Library could not tell us in what months the city directories gathered data or were published. However, the 1940 *Directory* has February 12 stamped, probably the date the library received it. A published disclaimer in the front states that the publishers could not guarantee the correctness of all the infor-

mation given to them in the actual canvas of residents. In addition, both the Davenport and Des Moines Public Libraries told us that their cities did not publish city directories in the early 1940s for one or two years. Presumably this was to save paper and, thereby, contribute to the war effort.

- Later data from the ELCA archives in Chicago contradict the information about church size, as reported in the *Des Moines Tribune* for January 1942. Certainly, St. John's was a very large Lutheran church, but statistics from the *ULCA Yearbook* for that year stipulate that Kountze Memorial in Omaha was, in fact, the largest such church in the country with a membership of 6,649. North Austin was second with 5,164 members, and St. John's in Des Moines fourth at 4,386. Since the newspaper article was written in January and the *ULCA Yearbook* presumably came out a year later, that may account in part for differences in stated and actual rankings. In any event, Weertz's emphasis on evangelism and growing the church is born out by the fact that from 500 members in 1925, when he came to Des Moines, the church had expanded over eight times that number in seventeen years.

- Trying to find Gruhn's assignments during the war, and through him Aunt Dot's whereabouts, proved especially challenging. The National Personnel Records Center in St. Louis sustained a fire in the early 1970s. Almost all army records were burned. Although the center has tried to reconstruct the files of military personnel to some degree, it was not possible to get the duty assignments and dates for Gruhn and Gene.

In this photo from the 1930s, Aunt Dot looks dressed for traveling. Note the length of the skirts. Also, women always wore hats when dressed up.

CHAPTER FIVE

Tracing an Army Chaplain's Wife

No wife wants to see her husband go off to war. Despite that Gene would be in the army medical corps and Gruhn was applying for the army chaplaincy corps, Caroline and Aunt Dot would still, no doubt, have been concerned that, at some time, their husbands might be on the front lines of fighting as they ministered to wounds, illness, suffering, grief, and what was then called shell shock. But, given the universal patriotism prevailing in the country after the attack on Pearl Harbor, both wives would have supported their husbands' desire to volunteer for the army. Although Gene had to have his hernia repaired before the army would accept him, Gruhn had several other requirements to fulfill before the army chaplaincy corps would accept him.

To what degree Gruhn's haste in applying for the chaplaincy was triggered by being out of a job or the patriotic fervor after Pearl Harbor is an open question. Probably both realities entered into his behavior. His final pay from the church was due on February 15. Aunt Dot was not working outside the home. Thus, no more money was coming in after mid-February. Not surprisingly then, Gruhn was well on his way toward fulfilling his application requirements for the chaplaincy by February 10.

After verifying his U.S. citizenship, he had to apply to the National Lutheran Council (NLC) in New York City for their endorsement. An application form he completed and dated February 10 says that he stood six feet tall and weighed 186 pounds. His parents, his education, and previous work at St. John's, as well as other skills/activities are all listed. In particular, he spoke German and had experience in radio singing as well as three years of violin study. He checked married as opposed to single but said nothing about his wife, not even her name or how long he had been married. By contrast, he gave a detailed account of his work with boys' and mens' organizations, both in Minneapolis and in Des Moines. In addition, he wrote a narrative history of his life to that date, in which he cited offices held in Luther League when in his teens and work done at Hollywood Lutheran Church in California prior to his Carthage College years. After covering his seminary years and work in Minneapolis, he concluded with his pastoral duties at St. John's Church where he had been "specializing in the work of evangelism, men's and youth organizations. During this time the net membership accession of St. John's totaled over 1,400 in four years." Gruhn's narrative gave the clear impression that he was the person primarily responsible for such astounding growth.

On the application form that the NLC required him to complete, he was asked to give the names and addresses of four representatives of the Iowa Synod, ULCA, who could recommend him for the chaplaincy. He was also asked to provide the names and addresses of five additional persons who could write letters of recommendation for him. Gruhn's file has seven additional letters of recommendation, all of which paint him as an outstanding candidate for the chaplaincy corps.

On February 12, Gruhn wrote to Dr. Ralph Long, chairman of the Lutheran Chaplaincy Committee of the NLC, to clarify that all requirements had been met except the needed endorsement of the Council. Gruhn also stated that he had, a few days earlier, met with Colonel Purdy in Omaha. This officer had declared "900 men" were needed right away in the chaplaincy corps. Then, in an effort to expedite his own application, Gruhn gave Dr. Long the names of eight more men who could recommend his candidacy.

On February 25, Gruhn wrote again to Long to find out the progress of his application. He again repeated that all other requirements had been met. He asked if the delay in his endorsement was due to a quota system. He also pointed out that he was being urged by a young mission church in Chicago, Edgebrook Lutheran, to accept a call to their congregation. Long wrote Gruhn on February 26 that no quota system existed in the processing of the chaplaincy applications. It was simply a matter of the appropriate committee doing their work carefully. Finally on March 5, Gruhn learned that the Committee on Army and Navy Work of the ULCA had given him denominational endorsement. Addressed to the Corps Area Chaplain of the Seventh Corps Area Headquarters in Omaha, Nebraska, the letter said:

> After careful investigation the National Lutheran Council herewith approves and endorses the application of the

> Rev. August Wilfrid Gruhn, St. John's Lutheran Church, Des Moines, Iowa, for appointment as a Reserve Chaplain in the U.S. Army and commends him to you for favorable consideration.

The letter was signed by Ralph M. Long as Executive Director of the NLC.

Gruhn's completed application had been received by the council on February 10. His endorsement came less than one month later. A reasonable interpretation of this length of time suggests that the committee had many applications to consider, and they were taking their work very seriously, giving all due diligence to the quality of men applying for the chaplaincy corps. Yet, with 900 men needed almost at once, the committee probably worked at breakneck speed to send the needed chaplains into the armed forces. It seems unlikely, though, that every candidate who applied for endorsement to the chaplaincy corps had the sterling credentials which characterized Gruhn.

In view of his private treatment of Aunt Dot, it seems appropriate here to quote from the several letters of recommendation for Gruhn in order to establish clearly his public image as painted by those who knew him in the seminary and in Des Moines by the spring of 1942. All those writing in his behalf were men, including: the President of the Iowa Synod; one pastor from Des Moines; two pastors from outside the city; the Dean of Northwestern Seminary in Minneapolis; three attorneys from Des Moines; a Vice President of a bank and trust in Des Moines; a state procurement officer for the treasury department, also in Des Moines; and a general agent for a life insurance company in Des Moines. The fragments quoted below pertain to Gruhn's character and behavior as known by these men during the four-and-a-half years he had served St. John's Church. No letter is quoted from twice; each paragraph is from a separate letter:

> Rev. Gruhn has a commanding personality and is a man of Christian character and integrity. He has a pleasing way of approaching people and wins confidence readily. He is a preacher of real ability and is evangelical in all his . . . pronouncements. He is also one hundred percent AMERICAN.

> During his stay in Des Moines he has won wide popularity not only within St. John's congregation but throughout the city. . . . He is a good student, a fine preacher, and his character and reputation are of the highest moral order.

The Rev. A.W. Gruhn . . . is one of the most energetic, aggressive, and able young men in the middle west. He is a consecrated, competent ambassador of the Lord, Jesus Christ.

He is admired and respected by the members of the church, his fellow pastors, and the people of the community. . . . I feel confident that he is the type of man who will win and hold the admiration of the men in the army.

Because of his scholarship and his varied and successful experiences in the pastorate since his graduation, I consider him exceptionally well qualified for the work of a chaplain.

He has an exceptional personality, is exceedingly well liked by all those who know him. . . . He enjoys the finest of reputations. . . .

Rev. Gruhn is eminently qualified by training and experience for the service he seeks and is richly endowed with those traits of character and personality qualifying him for spiritual leadership.

His character is above reproach, and he is eminently fitted by training, education, and personality to act as an army chaplain.

He is a young man of excellent character [and] exceptional ability. . . . Having served in the Army in the last war, I feel qualified to state that this young man would do honor to his country. . . .

I know a number of young men from St. John's Lutheran Church now enlisting in the army, including my own son, who are happy to know that Reverend Gruhn intends to serve as Chaplain in the Armed Forces.

In my opinion, Reverend Gruhn is a man of character and principle, he is honest and courageous and deeply sincere.

It goes without saying that Aunt Dot would not have found a man in Des Moines who would have believed her story about Gruhn's private treatment of her in their own house. How then do we reckon Aunt Dot's black eye with the man who evoked such sterling references from churchmen who knew him? Did men in general and clergy in particular accept as their divinely appointed right that they were the head of the household and could treat women as their servants? Some did. A biblical passage has often been quoted to justify the role of men in the family. Gruhn would have been familiar with the passage from Ephesians:

> Wives be subject to your husbands as you are to the Lord. For the husband is the head of the wife just as Christ is the head of the church, the body of which he is the Savior. Just as the church is subject to Christ, so also wives ought to be, in everything, to their husbands (Ephesians 5:22-24 NRSV).

The above verse has often been quoted. Much less often has the verse following been quoted:

> Husbands, love your wives, just as Christ loved the church and gave himself up for her, in order to make her holy by cleansing her with the washing of water by the word. . . . In the same way, husbands should love their wives as they do their own bodies (Ephesians 5:25-28 NRSV).

Depending upon a man's psychological make-up, he might have used the first quotation from Ephesians as license to treat his wife any way he felt at any given moment. Another man, more moderate in temperament, might have taken a much less literal interpretation of the biblical passage and also accounted for the second verse which laid responsibility on the male for the well-being of the marriage relationship. Still other men may have reasoned only from societal norms at the time and assumed that, of course, they held the superior position in the home.

Regardless of how the several kinds of male personalities interpreted their role in home and community, there is no question that it was men who went to fight the war, men who fulfilled the role of chaplain, and men who served as doctors in the war. Trying to find out what Aunt Dot did while Gruhn was in the armed forces has been difficult. Tracing what Caroline did when Gene was in the army medical corps has been easier, due to cousin Nancy's memory of family history. The two sisters-in-law had lived near each other in the historic district of Des Moines for a little over a year. When their husbands joined the army, they, like many wives, tried to follow their men when it was possible.

Gruhn and Gene would both have entered the army as officers, either Second or First Lieutenants. That meant they would have been accorded more privileges and more pay than enlisted men. Their wives would, therefore, have had money to live on without going to work while their husbands were in the service. Both Gruhn and Gene also had to fulfill some type of basic training pertaining to army protocol for officers, as well as specific training for a chaplain and for a medical doctor. Gruhn was assigned to Fort Benjamin Harrison in Indiana for his basic training. Gene probably went to Carlisle Barracks in Pennsylvania, since that was the typical place at the time for officers in the medical corps. Following their approximately six weeks of indoctrination into army regulations and officer responsibility, both men were assigned to their respective duty stations depending on what the needs were for the chaplaincy and the medical corps. Church records give us further information about where Gruhn and Aunt Dot were in the remaining months of 1942.

After serving in the chaplaincy corps for a year, Gruhn wrote to officials and clergy of the Iowa Synod to tell them what assignments he had received following his induction on April 27, 1942. These synod officials had written to him about a year later, on April 14, 1943, and Gruhn was responding to that "very welcome letter."

Having completed the chaplains' training school at Fort Benjamin Harrison, Gruhn was assigned to the "71st Observation Group, an Air Corp [sic] Unit, at Salinas, California." Although Gruhn had been inducted into the army, he was assigned to an air corps unit. That seems odd today, but at that time, the air corps was part of the army, not a separate division of the armed forces as it is today. Consequently, the designation AAF sometimes appears on Gruhn's papers, indictating Army Air Force.

Gruhn felt that the work of chaplains was "highly regarded in our Government and Armed Forces." He ministered to a congregation of officers and enlisted men, all of whom he felt were sincere and "highly responsive." He also told his former clergy colleagues in Iowa that the most difficult times for him were when training accidents occurred at this air force base:

> Young men with whom you have fellowship one hour, may be in that wreckage a hundred miles away the next. . . .
> At times like these the Chaplain's duty brings him to the home to notify an unsuspecting wife or mother. These are the times when Hell becomes naked before your eyes.

Gruhn spent thirteen weeks in the Mojave Desert, where the mid-summer temperature reached 130 degrees on a daily basis, before being transferred to his next assignment.

Gruhn does not mention Aunt Dot joining him in Salinas, in this letter to his former clergy colleagues of the Iowa Synod, but her membership card at St. John's Church indicates that she followed him to California. On that card, her address for 1942 says "Army Air Base—Obsn. Airdrome Salinas, Calif." No month is listed for her change of residence. However, an article in the *Des Moines Register* for June 24, 1942, on what was probably called the "society page," gave short notes on several local women and their activities. The update on Aunt Dot stated:

> Mrs. August W. Gruhn, 810 Hickman Road, left recently to join Lieutenant Gruhn at Salinas, Cal. where he is chaplain at the air base.

Assuming basic training of about six weeks, Aunt Dot followed her husband to Salinas soon after he was located there. From Gruhn's letter we have no insight into whether he and Aunt Dot lived together or how often they had private time together.

In his letter to former Iowa colleagues, Gruhn wrote that his next assignment after the heat of the Mojave Desert came in January 1943. His "unit moved into maneuvers at Alexandria [sic], Louisiana, where we spent another two months." At the end of March they were transferred to Laurel, Mississippi, for five days. Then Gruhn received individual orders that took him to Drew Field in Tampa, Florida, to the Aircraft Warning Unit Training Center. "This new responsibility brings me into an executive work, assisting other Chaplains make their start in their organizations." He closed his letter with positive thoughts about his own work and that of the chaplaincy:

> There is a vast opportunity for religion that we all feel we must give ourselves to—day and night. Indeed, I have no doubt but what the Armed Forces have become America's greatest mission field. Men are turning their hearts and minds toward God each day. There is a wholesome regard for things spiritual. Many men are being led into the presence of Almighty God daily.

Nowhere in this letter to Iowa clergy does Gruhn say that Aunt Dot traveled to be with him after California, to Louisiana and Mississippi. Indeed, there is no mention of even any letters that the two might have exchanged. But we do know that she, like many military wives, made great efforts to be near her husband.

An article in the *Des Moines Register* for August 22, 1943, tells a bit of the story. The title reads "Join Army Husbands and See the Country!" A Mrs. I. P. Wingert Jr. is pictured with her bag of golf clubs over her shoulder as she steps onto the running board of her car. A Des Moines resident, Mrs. Wingert is portrayed as "Mrs. America of '43" who "performs her wartime duties, keeps home intact as her husband remembers it, or provides a home for him wherever she can. To many wives, home actually is where they hang their hats, and they find themselves on domestic maneuvers near any number of army camps." Somehow Aunt Dot managed to catch a ride with Mrs. Wingert when the latter was travelling from her husband's previous assignment in California to Alexandria, Louisiana:

> Mrs. August Gruhn, wife of the Rev. Mr. Gruhn, formerly of Des Moines, accompanied Mrs. Wingert on the trip to Alexandria. They were delayed for a bit when they created an obstacle course for fighting men in desert warfare . . . with, of all things, a flat tire!

Mrs. Wingert laughed when she recalled: "Suddenly more than 100 soldiers swarmed around us to fix the flat."

Once in Alexandria, the rooming situation was described by Mrs. Wingert as "desperate." The women "haunted the USO rooming service." Sometimes they had a room guaranteed for only one night, so many women were trying to be near their husbands. But being near their husbands meant just that; it did not mean being *with* one's husband. Mrs. Wingert's husband was an officer, like Gruhn, but that did not mean special privileges in this situation. She saw her husband only three times during the ten weeks he was stationed in Alexandria. Then she followed him on to Laurel, Mississippi. Captain Wingert was the same rank and probably in the same army unit as Gruhn; they both had received the same postings, from Salinas to Alexandria to Laurel.

We have to assume that Aunt Dot probably saw Gruhn no more often than Mrs. Wingert saw her husband. However, Aunt Dot may have been able to hear Gruhn speak at a local church or for an evening chapel service on the base at which the soldiers were stationed. We can also assume that Aunt Dot spent her free time as Mrs. Wingert did—in volunteering for the USO and the Red Cross. To paint a more vivid picture of the housing crunch all over the country where men of the armed forces were stationed, we can look at Gene and Caroline's situation in these early years of the war.

Following his basic training, which ended sometime in late 1942, Gene was assigned to Walter Reed Army Hospital in Washington, D.C., for further medical training. Cousin Nancy remembers that her mother, Caroline, travelled with Gene to Washington. In later years, she described to Nancy their rather unusual living arrangement. Gene and Caroline managed to secure a studio apartment, consisting of one room with a single bed, a bathroom, and small kitchenette. Husband and wife alternated their times sleeping in the bed. Since Gene worked nights at the hospital, Caroline slept in the bed during his work hours. Gene slept in the bed during the daytime hours.

Sometime in early 1943, perhaps about the time that Gruhn was assigned to Drew Field in Tampa, Florida, Gene was ordered to Fort Sam Houston in San Antonio, Texas. More specifically, he trained at Brooke Army Medical Center. According to cousin Nancy's recollection, it was in San Antonio that Gene and Caroline experienced living accommodations a bit more luxurious than in their Washington, D.C., studio arrangement. The army had taken over a local motor court, and married officers were allowed to stay in the cabins. Gene and Caroline's cabin included a small living room and bedroom, plus a kind of tiny bathroom and kitchen combination. One sink served both. A small table just fit under the kitchen window and accommodated two people. When a third person sat at the table, the back legs of that person's chair lodged in the shower stall. For a marriage to survive such restricted and crowded housing arrangements certainly required the spouses to communicate well and maintain a sense of humor.

Since Aunt Dot had no children, we have to rely on newspaper accounts to know of her presence or absence in Gruhn's life at this time. On June 5, 1943, *The Tampa Times* announced that Captain August W. Gruhn would be speaking at the Sunday morning service of St. Paul Lutheran Church, a congregation of the ULCA. In the same paper for September 6, a sad note was printed:

> Chaplain August W. Gruhn, of Milwaukee, senior chaplain of the Air Warning Unit Training Center at Drew Field for the past five months, has received word that his brother, Lt. Paul Gruhn, 23-year-old Flying Fortress pilot, is missing in action following a recent bombing mission over Nazi-occupied Europe.
>
> On May 24, Chaplain Gruhn pinned the pilot's wings on his brother at Waco, Texas, where Lt. Gruhn was a member of the graduating class of the Waco Army Flying School.

Activities on base which Gruhn helped to organize and participated in included a weekly chapel service. According to *The Tampa Daily Times* for October 9, 1943, "One feature on Drew Field's Sunday calendar that packs a capacity audience is the Evening Chapel Hour," which included "several nationally known artists in its cast." On Saturday, November 20, *The Tampa Tribune* reported that the Sunday evening chapel hour would be dedicated to the nurses stationed at the field station hospital. "The program has been arranged by Chaplain A.W. Gruhn, senior AWUTC chaplain, and Corp. Arnold Felton, program director." On February 6, 1944, *The Tampa Tribune* printed a picture of Gruhn and several ladies, including Aunt Dot. The caption read:

> Each Sunday evening after the "A. W. Chapel Hour," Chaplain August W. Gruhn signs passes for civilian members of the audience so that they may leave Drew field and return to their homes in Tampa.

Aunt Dot is one of seven women receiving such passes.

Several weeks later, on Sunday, March 26, 1944, *The Tampa Tribune* reported that Gruhn's sister, Miss Esther Gruhn, first cellist with the Philadelphia Opera Company, was to play that evening at the "A. W. Chapel Hour." Another paragraph revealed that Esther had been visiting her brother, who by then had been promoted to Major and was called the "senior chaplain" of the Aircraft Warning Unit Training Center, and his wife, who was then living at 45 Davis Boulevard, about seven miles from the base. The language sounds like only Aunt Dot lived at that address, thus corroborating the caption and picture from February when Gruhn was shown handing out passes to civilians to leave the base and return home.

Sometime in May 1944, Gruhn left for San Antonio. He had served just over a year at Drew Field and was now assigned to a new type of chaplains' school at Lackland Air Base. According to the base periodical, *The Tale Spinner*, the training program being initiated was unique:

> The new two-week course, the only one of its kind in the armed services, indoctrinates Army chaplains and their assistants . . . into the Army Air Forces. It was officially inaugurated here June 15, as a unit of the Central Flying Training Command, AAF Training Command.[25]

Subjects to be covered in this "refresher course" included discharge of duties and office procedures, AAF organization and perspective, venereal disease control measures, leadership and "the art of counseling."

---

[25] *The Tailspinner* 3 (June 29, 1944):front page.

Chaplain Major August Gruhn, *of Davenport, Iowa,* (italics mine) was one of the initial six instructors for the school, according to *The Tail Spinner* article. All AAF chaplains were required to take this course, even those serving abroad, when their assignments brought them into the continental United States. To help publicize this new school, articles were sent out around the country via the Religious News Service.

We know that Gruhn probably stayed in San Antonio until June 1945, and we can assume that he stayed on the air base during those months. We do not know if Aunt Dot followed him to San Antonio. The fact that he is identified in *The Tail Spinner* as being from Davenport suggests that Aunt Dot was living there at the time. However, no Dorothy Gruhn was found in the city directories for either 1944 or 1945. We do know for sure that Aunt Dot would not have followed her husband to San Antonio in the hope of being near her brother and wife.

Although Gene and Caroline had been stationed there since spring of 1943, they were already gone from that city by the time Gruhn was assigned there. Gene had been ordered to the Pacific for duty in early February 1944. Caroline delivered her first baby in late February, all alone, though aided by an army doctor. Gene sat in a ship in San Diego and could not get leave to go home for the birth of his son. Caroline took the newborn and drove home to her mother's house in Moline, Illinois, next door to Rock Island and across the river from Davenport. She lived there until Gene was discharged from the army at the end of the war.

Absent more newspapers becoming digitized and available for search, the only other source we have for Aunt Dot is the archive at St. John's Church in Des Moines. Her communion record gives some perspective but does not fully clarify her whereabouts. It was typical at that time for the Lutheran church to commune members four times a year and to record the names of communicants. Aunt Dot's record says that she took communion out of town during the last two quarters of 1942, during all of 1943, and in the first quarter of 1944. A small "OT" is written in by each of the entries. During the remaining three quarters of 1944 she is recorded as taking communion, but no "OT" is written in. The same record holds for 1945. Either Aunt Dot wrote St. John's that she had communed or the church at which she had participated wrote to the Des Moines church. It is, of course, also possible that there were recording errors on her communion record.

We know from the newspaper articles cited above that Aunt Dot followed her husband around the country from June 1942 until late March

Tracing an Army Chaplain's Wife | 97

1944 when she was living in Tampa at 45 Davis Boulevard. If she went home to Davenport when Gruhn was sent to San Antonio, she may have thought that the hassle of travel and finding yet another place to lay her head was simply not worth the effort. By the end of March 1944, she had been following Gruhn around the country for one year and nine months. Husband and wife may have been able to live together, or he may have chosen or been required to live on base. The amount of private time they shared together would have been minimal, given Gruhn's desire to fulfill his duties. Maybe he told Aunt Dot not to follow him to San Antonio. He had been getting assignments and promotions that continued to paint a glowing public image. That may have been all he needed.

By the spring of 1945 the war had changed internationally for the United States and individually for Gruhn. Fighting in Europe had ended on May 7, when Germany signed the unconditional surrender document—VE Day. However, the United States was still involved in a large-scale conflict in the Pacific. Gruhn was ordered back to Drew Field in Tampa by June 1945. His time there was very short; he was about to get his wish for an expanded field of service.

When Gruhn wrote to his former Iowa colleagues in May 1943, he described his assignment at Salinas. He also noted, with what sounded like a tone of regret, that he and his unit had "narrowly *missed the privilege* of overseas service" (italics mine.) In July 1945, he finally got his desire for service abroad. Chaplain Gynther Storaasli, Gruhn's commanding officer, ordered him to the China–Burma–India Theater.

For brief insight into what this veritable cauldron of military and political intrigue amounted to, we can look at the first-hand analysis written by Theodore White and Annalee Jacoby in their book titled *Thunder Out of China*, published in 1946. The two constituted the Chunking bureau for *Time* magazine in the war years. In particular, White had arrived in China in 1939. Among other assignments, he flew with the 14th Air Force and the Hump Command, the larger group to which Gruhn was assigned.

According to White, the China–Burma–India (CBI) Theater had been set up by the American government in the spring of 1942, for the purpose of keeping China in the war. As with many plans that can look good on paper, the actual reality was a very different story. In White's graphic description:

> The CBI command was the stuff of legends; Americans used to say that you needed a crystal ball and a copy of

Alice in Wonderland to understand it. No Hollywood producer would dare film the mad, unhappy grotesquerie of the CBI. It had everything—maharajas, dancing girls, war lords, head-hunters, jungles, deserts, racketeers, secret agents. American pilots strafed enemy elephants from P-40s. The Chinese Gestapo ferreted out beautiful enemy spies in our own headquarters and Japanese agents knifed an American intelligence officer in the streets of Calcutta. Chinese war lords introduced American army officers to the delights of the opium pipe; American engineers doctored sick work elephants with opium and paid native laborers with opium too. Leopards and tigers killed American soldiers, and GI's hunted them down with Garands. Birds built their nests in the exhaust vents of B-17s in India while China howled for air power. Parties stomped over the silver floors of maharajas' palaces to the sound of boogie-woogie. . . . The U.S. Navy undertook to train a cavalry corps on the fringe of the Mongolian desert; it also trained the dread State Police of China in the techniques of the F.B.I. American experts taught Chinese everything from potato-growing to the newest methods of artificial insemination.[26]

The ostensible goal of CBI was to "supply China, retrain, re-equip, and regroup her armies, and send them out once more to fight the Japanese. . . . It was an essential mission." However, as White wrote, the CBI constituted both political and military theater. The several sides were divided into Chiang K'ai-shek and the Communists for China; the British and the Indians for India; plus our government and military staff for America. Any of the three entities could foul up the CBI plan of operations at any time. None of this was known to the average GI:

> He lived on bad food, in stinking rat-infested Chinese hostels; he had to fight off heat, mud and disease. No one bothered to explain to him what the War was about. All he knew was what lay within the routine of his daily life—and he hated it.

The "Hump" referred to the route flown by the American airplanes. To get from India to Kunming in China, they had to fly over the Burma mountains. For two or three years, the Kunming airport was "one of the

---

[26] Theodore H. White and Annalee Jacoby, *Thunder Out Of China* (New York: William Sloane Associates, Inc., 1946), 145-6.

busiest on the globe," according to White. "It handled most of the Hump traffic, all Chinese civilian traffic, the Chinese National Airlines' commercial carriers, the courier and mail services, and combat missions of the Fourteenth Air Force." Kunming was 6,000 feet high and the "main port of entry for all Americans into China."[27]

Gruhn would have flown into Kunming and probably found some of what White described had formerly characterized this city. It had been one of the national strongholds for opium traffic. Prostitutes were rampant. Indeed, White called it a "medieval cesspool." But by the time Americans landed, the city had been cleaned up a bit, to manage an air of respectability. Nonetheless, entertainment was limited to commercial sex, going to old and bad movies, playing poker for stakes, or "getting drunk."[28]

Certainly, seminary and St. John's Church in Des Moines had not prepared Gruhn for this type of environment. Even his civilian duties on military bases in the United States could not have prepared him for this Chinese cauldron. His new assignment in CBI carried the title of supervising chaplain. His parish in the stratosphere extended from Karachi east to Singapore and south to Java. So he was not counseling front-line soldiers but supervising and advising other chaplains who, in turn, counseled and held services for the individual GI.

Again, we are left to wonder about Aunt Dot. In their divorce papers, she testified that she had moved to Tampa in July 1945 and intended to take up permanent residence there. It seems likely she had learned that Gruhn had returned or was returning to Drew Field from San Antonio. She then made plans to return to Tampa to be with him permanently. No one knew how long the war in the Pacific would last, but clearly it was winding down. However, since we do not know the date in July when Aunt Dot arrived in Tampa, she might have connected briefly with Gruhn or missed him entirely. His DD 214 form, "Report of Separation" and "Certificate of Service," says he left the U.S. on July 23 and arrived in Calcutta on July 31.

Chaplains were needed in the Far East, given so many soldiers were still stationed there with no absolute certainty as to a final end of fighting. Gruhn may have asked for an order overseas or he may have been

---

[27] White, 159-60. In subsequent research, Kimberly Tucker was able to talk with the daughter of Gruhn's second wife. Among other recollections, this daughter recalled that Gruhn liked to brag about being the only chaplain who had flown over the "Hump" 40 times.
[28] White, 160-2.

assigned there, based on his prior excellent record. Indeed, Gynther Storaasli, his commanding officer, said later that Gruhn had been "outstanding" during the three years he served under Storaasli. As it turned out, hostilities ceased in August 1945, with the Japanese surrendering after the dropping of the atomic bomb on Hiroshima and Nagasaki. September 2, when Japan signed the surrender documents, has been known as VJ Day ever since.

However, the CBI did not close until June 1946. So Gruhn's assignment in the Far East extended for almost a year. Not least among the extraordinary activities that he would have been involved in was the active desire of India for independence. We do not know what his time spent in India versus China or points farther east amounted to, but certainly during 1946 in India there were large gatherings, if not riots, that he would have experienced.[29]

When CBI closed, Gruhn was transferred to the European theater with a similar supervisory position in the air force chaplaincy. America still had troops there to help maintain the peace and restore the war-devastated countries. An article in *The Lutheran* for February 26, 1947, is titled "C-54 pastor" and shows Gruhn stepping out of a plane in his uniform:

> Five years ago the Rev. August W. Gruhn called on parishioners by driving down Des Moines' Keosauqua Way. Now Major Gruhn makes his calls in a four-motored C-54—from Wiesbaden to Tripoli, Rome, Cairo, and Casablanca. He is chaplain for headquarters of the European Division of the air transport command. . . . Big as the major's present parish is, it is smaller than the China–Burma–India Theater, where he served until the command closed last June.[30]

After the peace treaty was signed in the Far East, most of the men in the armed forces were anxious to get home to the United States and to their loved ones. Cousin Nancy does not know in what month Gene came home, but she remembers that Caroline drove to the East Coast to meet him. From their 1945 Christmas card, we know he was home in time for the holidays. Husband and wife had written regularly during the almost two years of their separation. Gene had remained faithful to

---
[29] In additional research, Kimberly located Gruhn's third wife who confirmed that Gruhn had been profoundly affected by one riot he experienced in Calcutta.
[30] *The Lutheran* 29 (February 26, 1947):46

Caroline during their separation. A year after Gene's return home, they were overjoyed when Nancy Gene was born in October of 1946.

That very month Aunt Dot was experiencing what would trigger the final disintegration of her marriage. She learned that Gruhn wanted out. When he decided this, we do not know. Whether or not he wrote letters to Aunt Dot from CBI, we cannot tell. If he did not write to her very often, she would have wondered how long his duty in CBI would take. She probably hoped that he would be discharged in June 1946 when CBI closed. When he was then sent to Europe, she must have felt dispirited to have to continue the role of waiting wife. It seems unlikely she would have known that Gruhn would tell her of his decision to exit their marriage when he flew to the United States briefly for a chaplain's conference in October 1946. Following his bombshell of an announcement to Aunt Dot, he quickly returned to complete his remaining months of duty in Europe.

Clearly, Gruhn liked being in the military. But, given the end of the war and fighting men coming home, the number of chaplains was also being drastically reduced. For example, the Lutheran synod to which Storaasli belonged had eighty-three chaplains in the military in 1946; only eight remained on active duty in 1947.[31] Gruhn had no immediate future on active duty. Times had changed. Most people just wanted to get back to civilian life and normal routine as soon as possible.

Living by herself in Tampa beginning in July 1945, Aunt Dot had made sort of a wartime normal life for herself. She got a job as a clerk at the Tampa Municipal Hospital, not far from her apartment at 45 Davis Boulevard. Although Gruhn should have been sending her money to live on, she might have taken the job to earn extra money and to have a purpose in her daily life other than waiting for her husband. She could have spent her time in volunteer activities, but that might not have been sufficiently fulfilling for her. We do know that she made friends. In other words, she was not secluded and depressed. The *Tampa Tribune* for August 22, 1945, reports that Aunt Dot was one of several women assisting with a wedding reception for a young couple to be married at one of the Drew Field chapels. However, living by herself when the war was still on and her husband was assigned overseas was a different kind of single living than being alone every day and knowing that her husband no longer wanted to live with her.

---

[31] Lawrence J. Lystig, "The Military Chaplaincy Program of the Evangelical Lutheran Church 1917-1960" (Master of Theology Thesis, Luther Theological Seminary, 1977), chapter 4.

Aunt Dot had left college to be near Gruhn for the three years of his seminary study. She had taken care of his home, including moving at least four times in four years, when they lived in Des Moines. In those same years, she had suffered a black eye from his hand on at least one occasion that we can verify. She had followed him around the country during his military assignments between 1942 and 1945. She had waited for him while he was stationed in the Far East and Europe. When he came home for a few days in October 1946, after fifteen months abroad, and made his dramatic announcement, Aunt Dot must have felt totally betrayed. How did she respond?

Notes

- This chapter became a perfect example of how tracing Aunt Dot depended upon knowing Gruhn's whereabouts. Once we knew his assignment, Kimberly could then search digitized newspapers in the locale where Gruhn was stationed. Even though the National Personnel Records Center had lost most records due to fire decades ago, some of Gruhn's as well as Gene's military history was learned through their Bonus Case Files, which are available on the internet.
- Wartime Washington was so overcrowded that Hollywood even made a light-hearted comedy about living conditions. *The More the Merrier,* starring Jean Arthur, Charles Coburn and Joel McCrea, appears from time to time on Turner Classic Movies.
- City directories, telephone directories, plus available military records and base newspapers from Lackland Air Base in San Antonio have yielded no information about Aunt Dot. An officers' wives club did exist, but no records from that source have been found. Contact with military and base historians has been to no avail.

C-54 pastor FEB 26 1947

Five years ago the Rev. August W Gruhn called on parishioners by driving

down Des Moines' Keosauqua Way. Now Major Gruhn makes his calls in a four-motored C-54—from Wiesbaden to Tripoli, Rome, Cairo, and Casablanca. He is chaplain for headquarters of the European division of the air transport command.

Said the former pastor of St. John's Church, Des Moines, about the boys in his division: "These men overseas are better churchgoers than the folks back home. Soldiers here average about 30 per cent attendance."

Big as the major's present parish is, it is smaller than the China-Burma-India theater, where he served until the command was closed last June. There his units stretched from Karachi east to Singapore and south to Java.

Courtesy of ELCA Archives

CHAPTER SIX

Desertion, Then Divorce

At some point in time, Aunt Dot asked Gruhn for a written statement that he wanted out of the marriage. She may have asked him at the time he told her in person that he was leaving her. Or, she might have contacted a lawyer who told her to make such a request. Gruhn complied, though perhaps a bit tardily. His brief letter to her is dated January 2, 1947, and was mailed from Europe where he was then stationed. The letter has been preserved as Exhibit A in their divorce proceedings and reads as follows:

> Dear Dorothy:
>
> For reasons which you no doubt already know, I left you on or about October 1, 1946, and did not ever intend to return, and do not now ever intend to return to you as a husband.
>
> Very truly yours,
> August W. Gruhn

When I read his brief letter, it put a completely different light on Gruhn's allegations about Aunt Dot's behavior, as those were stated here in chapter one. As I carefully analyzed and digested all the contents of their divorce file, I came to realize that the allegations he had made to clergy officials in 1950, about Aunt Dot's unfaithfulness and their subsequent divorce, were all lies. A look at both parties' behavior between October 1946 and March 1948, when the divorce decree became final, presents a picture of each person that draws a stark contrast with their personalities as known in Des Moines.

Aunt Dot had, from October 1946 until Gruhn was discharged from the army and came home in September 1947, to decide what to do with her life. She may have hoped that he would change his mind about wanting out of the marriage, despite the definite tone of his letter of January 2, 1947. Nonetheless, she wrote to the church in Des Moines on

February 3, 1947, and sounded like the model wife who hoped that her husband would return soon from overseas duty:

> Greetings dear friends –
>
> It has been a long time since we have sent our best wishes to you all there, but we have thought of you—and that very often. Chaplain Gruhn is still overseas—Eleven months were spent in India, China, and Burma—now he is leaving Paris to spend some time in Germany—His days are well filled with a congregation that covers all of Europe and extends to Casablanca and Rome—Just when he will return to the States is very indefinite but we hope it will not be too many more months.
>
> We know that you will know to what use to put the enclosed check.

Aunt Dot wrote Gruhn's address at the end of the letter, and noted that her address was on the envelope. She signed it "Sincerely, D. Gruhn."

By not saying anything about their pending permanent separation, due to Gruhn's choice, she was protecting his image at their former church. She did not have to do that. But, she was also protecting her own image. She probably knew how tongues would wag among members of their former congregation if they learned that the marriage had not remained on solid ground. Given Gruhn's prior excellent reputation at the church, Aunt Dot would have been blamed for any failure in the marriage. According to her closing line, she sent a check to the church. She still retained her membership in Des Moines and, no doubt, felt an obligation to continue her tithe or smaller offering. She had been raised that way; even if money was tight, one still gave to the church. We can only guess at the conflicting emotions which may have overwhelmed her at times.

Gruhn may not have told her when his assignment in Europe would be over, but he came home in September 1947, having been formally separated from the army in Frankfurt, Germany. His final separation document says that he was granted some pay for travel in Europe before returning home to the States. Having written his letter saying that he was never coming back to live with her again, we do not know if he had been sending her monthly support. However, this final separation document says that he had one dependent.

From October 1946 until Gruhn came home in September a year later, Aunt Dot was facing an unknown and unexpected future. Yet she did not let that reality paralyze her. Tracing her life in those months, we can see that she made some significant decisions which propelled her forward into a new life. In the divorce papers, she states: "Over a year ago, when my husband left me, I decided to make my permanent home here in Tampa, Florida." She had no family nearby. But maybe she wanted to be far from her family. She might have felt like she had failed in the marriage. Compared to her older brothers and her parents, Aunt Dot may have felt like the "black sheep" in the family. Had she moved back home to Davenport, she would have faced questions, perhaps accusations, from all the family nearby.

Just when Aunt Dot also decided to divorce Gruhn, we can never know. In so doing, she made a momentous decision; for there had never been a divorce in the Wagner family. The decision cast her as a quiet rebel. It also cast her as a very strong woman. Gruhn's announcement that he was leaving her did not necessarily mean that he would eventually initiate divorce proceedings. Aunt Dot could have chosen to wait and see what he would do, thereby allowing him to, once again, be in command. She could also have chosen to live separately from him for the rest of her life; however, that would have left her married but living singly and being legally tied in many ways. Rather than remaining passive, she acted. She decided to initiate divorce proceedings and so hired a lawyer.

When I inititally contacted the Florida Office of Vital Statistics, after reading Gruhn's allegations about Aunt Dot's adultery, the one-page response I received clearly stated that Aunt Dot had been the plaintiff and the divorce was uncontested. That response made me want to find out the details of their divorce and thereby to ascertain the truth or falsehood of Gruhn's allegations. With Kimberly Tucker's personal presence and persistent requests at the office, I was eventually able to get the entire divorce file.

Just when and how Aunt Dot found her lawyer, Paul Lake, we also have no way of knowing. She would have engaged him at least by October 1947—probably a year earlier, when Gruhn told her he wanted out of the marriage. Aunt Dot would have had to learn about grounds for divorce in Florida. Clearly, being abroad on army assignment did not constitute desertion. She would also have learned that a divorce on the grounds of "willful, obstinate and continued desertion of complainant by defendant" could not be granted in less than one year's time.

On December 23, 1947, Lake presented the Bill of Complaint he had drawn up for Aunt Dot "TO THE HONORABLE JUDGES" of the Circuit Court, of the 13th Judicial Circuit in Florida. It lays out the grounds for divorce based on desertion and argues for alimony:

> That during all the time she lived and cohabited with the defendant, she demeaned and conducted herself as a true, loyal, and unselfish wife, striving at all times to make the defendant happy and contented.
>
> That on October 1, 1946, without cause or provocation, and without fault on the part of the plaintiff, the defendant did willfully, and obstinately desert the plaintiff and has remained apart from her since said date. Wherefore, the plaintiff charges that the defendant has been guilty of willful, obstinate, and continued desertion for more than one year last past and prior to the filing of this Bill of Complaint.
>
> Plaintiff further charges that she has no means or money with which to support herself during the pendency of this suit or thereafter; that she has no means or money with which to pay her attorney of record for the bringing of this suit and prosecution of this suit, or to pay the costs hereof; whereas the defendant is an able bodied man, well able to pay the temporary and permanent Court costs, and temporary and permanent alimony to the plaintiff.

On the same date, the petition was filed and docketed as "Divorce, etc. No. 80089—C." It was one of several suits filed with the Circuit Court, according to *The Tampa Tribune* for December 24. That date was ten years to the day from the time when Aunt Dot and August Gruhn had looked forward to their marriage ceremony in St. John's Lutheran Church, right after the Christmas Eve service.

Paul Lake had twenty years experience as an attorney. He had been admitted to the Florida Bar in 1927. According to his obituary, he had specialized in family and criminal law, and had no history of disciplinary action against him. Aunt Dot had a lawyer who was not only very experienced but also undoubtedly familiar with a variety of personalities and psychological profiles. Surely she would have told him of the abuse suffered as Gruhn's wife. However, even if she had not told him all of the private behavior she had endured, Lake would have queried her thoroughly as to her own behavior. Unfaithful spouses were not uncommon during the war years, and Lake had a professional reputation to maintain.

Although divorce at that time was more common than in prior decades, the number of marriages ending in divorce was not nearly what it is today and has been in recent decades. In addition to desertion, Florida law in 1947 permitted divorce only on limited grounds including: impotence, within degrees of relationship prohibited by law; adultery; desertion; habitual intemperance; extreme cruelty; bigamy; habitual indulgence in violent and ungovernable temper; or that the defendant had obtained a divorce from the plaintiff in another state or country.[32]

Of these choices, Lake prepared the case for Aunt Dot on the ground of willful desertion. He probably also advised the two parties to agree on a property settlement before going in front of a judge. Such an agreement, prepared in advance, could save both time and money. A look at what is called a "STIPULATION" in their divorce papers makes clear that Gruhn, as the defendant, assumed all dollar costs. The details of that "STIPULATION" included:

> Gruhn had to pay Aunt Dot $100 per month "until the full amount of Ten Thousand ($10,000) Dollars has been paid" or until Aunt Dot remarried.

> Gruhn had to give Aunt Dot all of her personal property, like household furniture, whether they were then stored in Des Moines, Davenport, or Tampa. And he had to ship such belongings "at such time, or a reasonable time thereafter, as the plaintiff shall make demand upon the defendant so to ship."

> Gruhn had to relinquish to Aunt Dot "all right, title, and interest in" precious or semi-precious stones, government bonds or any other bonds then in his possession .

> Gruhn had to pay Paul Lake $150 for attorney's fees and court costs.

> Gruhn had to file a joint income tax return for himself and Aunt Dot and to pay all costs due from such filing for the year 1947.

---

[32] Chapter 65 of Florida Law, "Divorce, Alimony and Custody of Children," section 65.04 "Grounds for divorce."

Gruhn had "appropriated to his own use a Buick automobile which was the sole and exclusive property" of Aunt Dot. Therefore, he had to pay her "an amount equal in money to the costs to the plaintiff of said Buick automobile."

This "stipulation" was signed by Aunt Dot and Gruhn on December 31, 1947. He had agreed to a heavy financial burden. Did he do so voluntarily? Or did Paul Lake threaten him with a lengthy trial and perhaps greater financial burden if he did not comply with this "STIPULATION" before appearing in court? When the case did come to court, the "STIPULATION" was entered as Exhibit B.

If Aunt Dot had indeed been unfaithful, as Gruhn had alleged, why then did he not become the plaintiff and sue her for divorce on the ground of adultery? Florida law permitted that. Moreover, the Lutheran church recognized divorce if the minister was the innocent party and the wife had been unfaithful. That was the ground on which Gruhn had written to church officials in 1950 and maligned Aunt Dot. It also seemed to me further evidence of her innocence that she was granted alimony, which extended out over eight years if she did not remarry. Florida law did not permit alimony to be granted to an unfaithful wife.[33]

As an experienced lawyer, Paul Lake queried Aunt Dot in sworn testimony before a judge about her behavior. He did so in the Circuit Court of Hillsborough County, Florida, on February 21, 1948:

> MR. PAUL LAKE, Solicitor for Plaintiff.
>
> BY MR. LAKE:
>
> Q Please state your name?
>
> A Dorothy Wagner Gruhn.
>
> Q Where do you live?
>
> A 45 Davis Boulevard, Tampa, Florida.
>
> Q How long have you lived in the State of Florida?
>
> A Since July 1945.
>
> Q Where do you live?
>
> A At the Casa Del Sol Hotel, Davis Islands, Tampa, Florida.
>
> Q Has that residence been continuous since then?
>
> A Yes, sir.

---

[33] Op. Cit., section 65.08.

Q What business are you engaged in?

A As a school teacher.

. . . .

Q What is your husband's name?

A August W. Gruhn.

Q When were you married to him?

A December 25, 1937.

Q Are you living with him now?

A No, sir.

Q When did you separate?

A October of 1946.

Q Tell us in brief, as near as you can, the cause of the separation.?

A He came home in October 1946, and he said he was leaving and he was not coming back.

. . . .

Q *Did you give your husband any cause or reason to leave you?*

A *No sir. I certainly did not.* [italics mine]

Q What kind of wife did you make him while you lived with him?

A A very good wife.

Q *Were you rather astonished that he was going to leave and not come back?*

A *Yes, sir, I was.* [italics mine]

Q Have you lived with him since then?

A No, sir, I have not.

Q Do you know of any reason why he should have left you and not returned?

A No, sir, I do not. I do not think that he wanted to be married.

Q That is the only reason?

A Yes, sir.

As additional strong evidence of Aunt Dot's innocence, we have her sworn declaration before a judge that she had never given her husband "any cause or reason" to leave her.

Paul Lake then called a character witness, Mary Bach. In sworn testimony, she stated that she lived at the Casa Del Sol Hotel and had known Aunt Dot since November 1946. She further confirmed that Aunt Dot had not lived with her husband in the time she had known her. Bach clarified that she would have known if Gruhn had been home, since she and Aunt Dot "work together in business and socially also. I see her frequently." When asked, "What kind of person is the plaintiff; do you think that she would be a person that would be a good wife?" Bach responded, "Oh, yes, I certainly think so, because she is very even tempered and very easy to get along with." For Mary Bach to have been brought in by Paul Lake as a character witness indicates that she and Aunt Dot had become very good friends. The relationship reminds us that Aunt Dot had also gone to a new city, Minneapolis, and made good friends with a total stranger, Viola Mathiowitz, who later became maid of honor at Aunt Dot's wedding. Thus, Bach's testimony rings true.

With no contesting the divorce by Gruhn, no children involved, and the "STIPULATION" drawn up in advance, the petition by Aunt Dot was quickly granted. On March 2, 1948, she became a divorced woman, and Gruhn became a divorced Lutheran minister.

Reading through legal documents tells what happened to people as a result of decisions and the law. Such reading does not tell about the emotions which may have engulfed Aunt Dot.

Actually having the divorce decree in hand would have given some sense of finality to the emotional struggles she would have been going through since Gruhn came home in October 1946 and announced that he was never coming back to live with her. However, the decree represented, not just the end of a civil marriage, but the death of a relationship which the Lutheran church had considered a sacred union ordained by God. Physical death of a spouse can leave the survivor feeling like one's insides are nothing but an emotional swamp. For Aunt Dot—having been raised Lutheran, having been discarded by her Lutheran minister husband, and having initiated the divorce proceedings within our secular legal system—she could also have felt like a tangled morass of emotions, including anger, guilt, failure. Yet, the months of living alone and making her own daily life decisions could have made it easier for her to move ahead into a new life.

In addition, Aunt Dot would have developed a deep emotional reservoir from her Wagner family that would have sustained her. Going back to her high school days in Davenport, she would have remembered that, when Grandpa lost everything but the house in 1928, none of the family had given up, gotten depressed, or turned to drink. They all turned to work. Aunt Dot might have remembered hearing about her paternal grandmother in Germany who had suffered abuse and desertion by an alcoholic husband and also lost six children, yet she pressed on, came to this country, and died at the ripe old age of 80 in 1916. Aunt Dot would certainly have recalled Grandma always carrying on with her household responsibilities, no matter what hardship prevailed on the family. Consciously or unconsciously, Aunt Dot would have absorbed the emotional drive from her parents and her older brothers to pursue her goals no matter what adversity life throws at you. Giving up, being lazy, and feeling sorry for herself simply would not have been in her inherited catalogue of acceptable behaviors.

Given this family background, Aunt Dot made further choices to forge ahead with her new life as a single woman. It seems very likely that Mary Bach introduced her to the Sherman K. Smith school for helping hearing-impaired children. Bach was an assistant at the school, also a single professional woman. Probably with Bach's encouragement and Aunt Dot's love of children, she began taking training in teaching hearing-impaired and deaf children how to speak. In addition, Aunt Dot chose to go back to college. When she entered the University of Tampa in September 1947, she was following in the tradition of her older brothers, all of whom had one or more graduate degrees. She was sacrificing like they had done to get those degrees. The death of her marriage had not pushed her into depression; it had prompted her to call forth all of the elements of resilience that had been essentially buried in her being.

Aunt Dot's positive behavior contrasts with that of Gruhn. He had, apparently, been a man of strong faith and belief in the Christian gospel. The recommenders in Des Moines who wrote on his behalf for entry into the chaplaincy in 1942 portrayed Gruhn as an ideal young minister who would make an excellent chaplain and give credit both to the Lutheran church and to the army chaplaincy. His military assignments under Gynther Storaasli, his commanding officer, had all been performed commendably. Gruhn knew that the ULCA disapproved of divorce, especially among clergy. Why then did he intentionally move to get out of his marriage?

At the time of his divorce, he well knew that he was behaving in a manner that his minister father, his minister brothers, and his clergy colleagues would consider sinful, and that would bring down censure on himself and disrepute on his family. Did he think that he could tell lies that would be believed? Was he experiencing a crisis of faith? His two younger brothers who had enlisted in the army had both been killed during the war. Could that knowledge, plus his recent experience in CBI, have pushed him to the realization that he had entered the ministry simply because that was expected of him by his family? He had been named after his father who was a minister, and he followed in the footsteps of his older brother who was also a minister. At the very least, we can say that Gruhn wanted out of his marriage because he found it unfulfilling.

One thing seems quite clear; Gruhn's decisions were always about himself. He had spoken persuasively for Aunt Dot to come to Minneapolis and wait for him while he finished seminary. Similarly, he had determined that their wedding should occur at midnight after the Christmas Eve service, when he could make her his trophy bride in front of a full church. Undoubtedly, Aunt Dot had concurred with his choices. But, ten years later, he alone had decided that he wanted out of the marriage. So he simply came home in October 1946 and announced that he was leaving her. He had decided to discard the woman that he had chosen to marry a decade before.

Questioning the behavior and choices of a veteran who had survived a world war was not an easy task. But for those men, like Gene, who had a sturdy and disciplined home life growing up, followed by a marriage which felt like it was made in heaven, settling into civilian life at the end of the war was easier. As a physician serving in hospitals in New Guinea and the Philippines, Gene certainly had been exposed to tragedy and death of all kinds. But when he came home in late 1945, he had a wife and baby son with whom to reunite, as well as parents and brothers' families nearby. After a refresher medical course at the University of Iowa, he took over a practice in a peaceful small town with surrounding Iowa farms.

Although Gene and Aunt Dot had been close growing up and had lived near each other when Gene and Caroline moved to Des Moines, it is not known how much he understood of her relationship with Gruhn and their divorce. Calling long distance to Iowa in 1947 was costly. For Aunt Dot to have explained over the phone all that had gone on with Gruhn would have been well nigh impossible and prohibitive in terms of dollars.

When she came home to Davenport for a visit in the spring or summer of 1947, she would probably have told family some of what Gruhn had said to her. She may or may not have made up her mind to divorce him at that point. But she was already learning and working at the Sherman K. Smith school. That visit was when I asked her how she could teach a deaf child to learn to speak. I was in grade school but I remember distinctly that she put my hands at certain places on her throat and asked me to feel the changes in musculature or vibrations when she made certain sounds. So the method she was learning was one-on-one, tactile, intensely personal, and required amazing patience. As the next chapter will detail, it is clear that she was learning a new method of how to help hearing-impaired and deaf children not just to speak, but to speak with a normal voice quality.

Notes

- In order to have an outside objective observer analyze the divorce papers, I asked Kimberly Tucker to find a current practicing lawyer in Tampa who would review Aunt Dot's case. Although the lawyer had not read the allegations Gruhn made about Aunt Dot in 1950, he had been told about the content and the context, i.e. that Gruhn was trying to get back into the chaplaincy and needed clergy approval. After reviewing the divorce record, the lawyer wrote: "I believe any unbiased look at it would have to indicate that . . . he [Gruhn] had everything to gain by making those false statements about her. The court record totally contradicts his assertions."

Dot's photo at her graduation in 1951 from the University of Tampa. She graduated with a Bachelor of Science degree in Education, with a major in Elementary Eduation and a minor in English.

CHAPTER SEVEN

New Challenges

Although living is constant choosing, some choices are much more challenging than others—both making them and enduring the consequences. When people make tough intentional choices, it is usually because they have a sense of their own empowerment, i.e. a sense of "I can . . . ." or "I will. . . ." They have a goal and intend to move toward accomplishing that goal. When Aunt Dot hired Paul Lake and pushed ahead with divorce proceedings, began learning how to teach the hearing-impaired child, and applied to go back to college at the University of Tampa, I believe she knew, deep down, that she was smart and disciplined. But she was no braggart; she had been raised to let her actions speak louder than her words. In making these decisions to re-orient her life, Aunt Dot would have drawn on her emotional reservoir from the Wagner family, her previous college accomplishments, and the era in which she lived. By the late 1940s, women had been voting for almost three decades, had successfully filled men's jobs during the war years, and were gradually moving into ever more challenging professions.

In 1947, when Aunt Dot was 34 years old, with a failed marriage and no children, I think it never occurred to her that she might not succeed in any of her newly chosen endeavors. She may have suffered some anxiety, wondering how she would do in college classes with young students who had been used to studying and taking tests.[34] She certainly knew that she had to manage her time and money carefully in order to pay rent, utilities, and tuition. Moreover, she knew she had to work hard at Sherman K. Smith's school in order to learn his intensive technique of teaching deaf and hard-of-hearing children to speak. But I doubt that she ever seriously entertained the thought of failure. When you pursue goals of your own choosing, you release an energy and inner drive that

---

[34] Kimberly Tucker contacted the archivist at the University of Tampa to get an estimate of student body size for the academic year 1947-48. After the War, many men returned to college on the GI Bill. So Aunt Dot would not have been totally unique as an older student returning to college. According to the archivist, looking at yearbook pictures, a total of 238 students were enrolled, and approximately 42 appeared to be "older."

sustains you, no matter the momentary obstacles. In Aunt Dot's case, the satisfaction of gaining new knowledge and skills would have carried her through the tough times of little money and new academic rigors, as well as the down periods when she would have wondered if the marriage failure was her fault? If she had tried hard enough?

Tracing Aunt Dot in these new challenges, we gain a picture of her emerging pattern of resilience as a single, mature woman. In this journey it seems clear that Mary Bach played a critical role. Especially when we go through difficult emotional circumstances, we need a confidante and friend to walk with us—to listen, to encourage, to laugh, and to cry with us. Mary Bach must have filled that role of mentor and faithful friend.

We usually choose people as close friends when we find that we share common interests and background. Bach appears to have been a confident, single, professional woman teaching at the Sherman K. Smith school. She is listed on the school's literature in 1948 as his assistant, with an M.A. after her name. Like Aunt Dot, she came from Midwestern, German roots. Similarly, both sets of parents married very early in the twentieth century. However, Bach was the oldest child in her family, in contrast to Aunt Dot as the youngest in the Wagner family. Both women also had experienced the upheaval that comes with a family moving distances to a new location, due to job changes.

Born in 1907, Mary Bach grew up in North Dakota. Her father worked as a conductor on the Great Northern Railroad. Undoubtedly, that accounted for the fact that the family moved great distances. According to the 1910 census, the family lived in Devil's Lake, in the eastern part of the state. Ten years later, they lived on the western border of the state in Williston. In 1930, they were back in eastern North Dakota, in Fargo. Life was hard; affluence and flourishing city life were hard to achieve. There was, however, a state school for deaf people in Devil's Lake as early as the 1890s. Whether or not a young Mary Bach had some connection with that place, we do not know. But by 1934 an adult Mary Bach lived in St. Augustine, Florida, and was teaching at the Florida State School for the Deaf and Blind. Begun in the 1880s, the school had sixty-two students enrolled by 1892, graduated its first students in 1898, and continued to grow. The President's Biennial Report for 1934-1936 lists Miss Mary Bach, B.A. as one of eleven teachers who held a bachelor's degree. Several more names were listed as teachers of deaf students, but without a degree. Altogether twenty-four individuals taught the deaf students; six taught the blind students. Additional faculty and staff at the school constituted a Department of Physical Culture, a Department of Music, and a Domestic Department.

In tracing Bach's life and career through city directories, newspaper articles, and census data, we find that she moved to Tampa in June 1944. However, her previous affiliations with Sherman K. Smith suggest that she settled in Tampa due to her connections with him. For example, *The Tampa Bay Times* for January 2,1944, reports that she visited the city for the fiftieth wedding anniversary celebration of Smith's parents. In the *Tampa Tribune* on March 25, 1945, an article announces "Newcomer Buys Apartment House." Mary Bach had purchased an eight-unit apartment building for $10,000. Following the real estate announcement, the article explains that Bach had spent two summers in Tampa prior to moving to the city permanently. By the time of the apartment house purchase, Bach was teaching a "new class" of eight deaf children that Smith had started. The article also details the fact that Bach had served as Smith's assistant when he was on the faculty of Michigan State Teachers College, in a summer school position, probably in 1940 or 1941. In addition, the *Tribune* article notes that Bach had formerly served as head teacher of the Primary Department at the Tennessee School for the Deaf.

We know from Aunt Dot's divorce papers that Bach said she had known Aunt Dot since November 1946. That was one month after Gruhn came home briefly and told Aunt Dot he was leaving her. In a sense, Bach may have felt like a lifeline to Aunt Dot. As a single, professional woman, six years older than Aunt Dot, Bach would have projected confidence, stability, and service, especially when she told about her work at Sherman K. Smith's school.

Dr. Sherman K. Smith, Sc.D. and D. Mus., first listed his school for teaching the deaf and hard-of-hearing in the *Tampa City Directory* for 1947, although his obituary says that he first moved to Tampa in 1938. The class that Bach taught in 1945 may have been an expansion of teaching that Smith had begun on his own. In what appears to have been an annual advertisement in *The Volta Review*, a national publication, Smith's enterprise is called a "School of Speech and Oral Education for the Deaf, Hard of Hearing and Rehabilitation of Speech." In June of 1951 the University of Tampa recognized Smith's "original methods" by granting him their "citizen of the year" award. The student newspaper, *The Minaret*, for June 1, printed a lengthy sketch of Dr. Smith's background and his teaching methods:

Through the study of voices at the Conservatory of Music in Boston came a life long interest in the study of normal voice quality and how to produce it in the congenitally deaf child. He believes that sign language for the deaf isolates them from the hearing world. . . . While he was in Boston he studied the musculature of the voice and breathing mechanism, and found that there were no existing medical charts dealing with these special areas and it was on this work in making medical charts, and plaster models from his own dissection that he was given his Doctoral degrees. These charts are to be found in many of the leading universities including Cornell, the University of Chicago, University of California, and many others. From these charts, and a better knowledge of the function of speech he has devised a completely new method of teaching speech to the deaf.[35]

Dr. Smith had received voice training at the New England Conservatory of Music and Columbia University, according to his obituary in *The Tampa Morning Tribune* for September 3, 1954. As a result of his work there: "In 1917 he became interested in the development of teaching of speech and subsequently became a doctor of science of speech and a doctor of music at the Capital College of Oratory and Music at Columbus, Ohio." His work needs to be set in the then-prevailing context of teaching the deaf either to sign or to read lips. Smith's goal was always to help the deaf child speak with as normal a quality of voice as possible. Although he had his own school in Tampa, Smith had also served as a guest lecturer at several colleges and universities around the country.

Through a stroke of good fortune via internet searches, Kimberly Tucker came into contact with a former student of Dr. Smith. Mr. James Short was kind enough to share his personal experience of the methods which helped him learn to speak. In fact, little Jimmy Short, four years of age, was pictured on the page advertising Smith's school in *The Volta Review* for May 1949. The text accompanying the picture says that Jimmy came from Lebanon, Indiana, in September 1948. He entered the school with "no formal sounds." By May 1949, "Normal voice quality has been established." And Jimmy was using "one hundred words

---

[35] *The Minaret*, ". . . the official publication of the student body of the University of Tampa . . . is published bi-weekly during the school year. . . ." (June 1, 1951): 2.

or more."[36] Mr. Short's adult description of how Mary Bach taught him reminded me of the brief experience I had had long ago when I asked Aunt Dot how she taught a deaf child to speak. Writing to Kimberly Tucker in an email, Mr. Short recalled:

> She did hands to the throat to feel the vibrations and would get up close face to face and tell me to repeat each letter with an exaggerated movement of her mouth while I was holding my hand to her throat and have simple words on the blackboard and point to them and keep repeating them and having me do the same—a lot of repetition!

Further commenting on Bach's approach, Mr. Short recollected: "She demanded excellence and, looking back, I appreciated her for that. She brooked no nonsense from anyone."

Additional testimony to the success of Dr. Smith's method and Mary Bach's teaching skill comes from a feature article in *The Tampa Daily Times* for September 29, 1956. Smith had died two years earlier, but parents managed to get support for opening a new private school, the Gulf Coast School of Oral Education, with Bach as principal and teacher. Pupils at the school had all originally been students at Sherman K. Smith's school. The "ultimate aim" of this new Gulf Coast School was to "put each deaf child into a public school with hearing children as soon as possible. One parent of a deaf boy who received instructions at the school has seen this goal become a reality. The mother, Mrs. Lee Short, is now serving as teacher with Miss Bach in the oral school."

It is easy to see how Aunt Dot could have been captivated by listening to Mary Bach tell about Smith's school and methods. In her 1951 application to teach in the Hillsborough County School District, Aunt Dot wrote that she had always been interested in children and particularly in helping the handicapped child. So, at a time when she had been deserted by her husband, she learned of a program to do just that. Trying to piece together the next five years of Aunt Dot's life makes clear that she performed a veritable juggling act in order to accomplish her goal.

We have no definite records for Aunt Dot for the remainder of 1946 after Gruhn told her in October that he was leaving her. Smith's school would very likely have been operating in the Casa Del Sol Hotel at that time, since it was listed there in the 1947 city directory. We can, there-

---

[36] *The Volta Review*, published by the Volta Speech Association for the Deaf, Alexander Graham Bell Association for the Deaf, and Alexander Graham Bell Association for the Deaf and Hard of Hearing (Washington, D.C.: Volta Bureau), n. pag.

fore assume that Aunt Dot may have started lessons to learn his teaching method at least by the start of that calendar year, but perhaps earlier. In her later application to teach in Hillsborough County, Dr. Smith is one of her references. He says there that he has known her both as a student and a teacher for about five years.

In order to have money to live on, Aunt Dot worked as a clerk at the Tampa Municipal Hospital, which was located not far from where she lived on Davis Island. She may have gotten that job in late 1945, when she moved to Tampa. After all, she had gotten a job at the Sears Store when she moved to Minneapolis, and at the Iowa Retail Sales Tax Division when she and Gruhn lived in Des Moines. So she was competent and unafraid to go out and look for a job in a new city. She is listed as a clerk at the hospital in both the 1946 and 1947 city directories. It is not known whether Gruhn had requested the army to send her support money out of his pay when he served in CBI and whether or not he had continued that practice once he had announced that he was leaving her.

The first half of 1947 probably continued as a time of emotional healing for Aunt Dot. In the process, she made another major decision. She had her transcript from Carthage College sent to the University of Tampa, applied for admission, and, by the start of fall semester, she was taking three three-credit courses at the university: Introduction to Education, Children's Literature, and Methods of Teaching Reading. These courses indicated that she had changed her mind about a major.

Although she had pursued a major in Home Economics when at Carthage, she decided on a degree in Elementary Education with a minor in English at the university. This change in majors suggests that Aunt Dot exercised her own independent choice as to her future direction. Following a Home Economics major at Carthage was a natural path, given Grandma's influence as an excellent homemaker. That path also led toward the societal ideal of wife and mother which prevailed in the 1930s. By changing to a major in elementary education, Aunt Dot was preparing herself to teach and to follow an ideal that she had always held, i.e. to help the child with special needs. No doubt her early work at the Sherman K. Smith school served to reinforce this decision to change majors.

Aunt Dot completed those first three courses of her new major, but no letter grades are given on her transcript. Numerical listings suggest that she finished in the B and C range. She probably wanted to get used to the routine of going back to classes after a thirteen-year absence from the classroom. Her transcript also says that she had initially signed up for a fourth course but withdrew from that on September 25, possibly finding the load too much for her first semester back in college. Her emotional struggles included not just a return to college but her upcoming final decisions and divorce from Gruhn. Honorably discharged from the army chaplaincy, Gruhn returned to this country in late September 1947, after having completed his assignment in the European Theater.

It is one thing to pursue a new life when the person who has wronged you is not present in your daily existence. When that person is visually present and does things which affect you dramatically, it is very disturbing. Sometime in late 1947, Gruhn appeared in Tampa and took Aunt Dot's automobile, which had been her sole and exclusive property. The divorce papers say that he "appropriated" it. Thus, her mode of transportation for getting to the hospital and to the university had to be altered—a great inconvenience. According to the divorce papers, Gruhn had to pay her for the cost of the car; still, she had to expend time and energy in getting a replacement. By the end of the fall term, Paul Lake had filed her divorce petition. By December 31, she and Gruhn had signed the "STIPULATION" for property settlement. On February 21, 1948, Paul Lake questioned Aunt Dot in sworn testimony and queried Mary Bach as a character witness. The divorce was final on March 2, 1948. Gruhn had to pay her alimony of $100 per month, starting immediately.

Aunt Dot also had some other income, but money would have been tight. According to her later application to teach in the Hillsborough County School District, she worked at Sherman K. Smith's school from 1947 to 1949. Her annual salary there was $1,300, though we have no months listed. This may have meant that she worked as a kind of intern or practice teacher, learning and doing some teaching at the same time. In addition, she had to pay tuition at the university, since she also enrolled in two courses for the spring semester of the 1947-48 school year. One course was titled Methods of Teaching Arithmetic, Spelling, and Handwriting in the Elementary School; the second was Methods of Teaching Music in the Elementary School. Despite emotions surrounding the divorce, Aunt Dot earned an A in one of these courses and an A- in the other. Given her time investment in the university courses and teaching at Smith's school, it seems highly unlikely that she could have continued, even part-time, with her hospital job. Thus, she would have been living on $2,500 per year, including alimony, or $208.33 per month to pay rent, utilities, food, tuition, transportation and miscellaneous expenses.

That summer of 1948, Aunt Dot took a course at the university from Dr. Smith. It carried three credits and was titled Methods of Teaching Language to the Deaf and Hard of Hearing. Copies of correspondence with university administrators indicate that Dr. Smith had hoped to become a regular faculty member, but that did not work out. This single course was the only one that Aunt Dot took from him at the university. In her application to teach in Hillsborough County, she states that her work with Dr. Smith was in addition to her regular college work.

In the fall term of 1948-49, Aunt Dot continued with two courses, but made another rather major decision. Her transcript from the University of Tampa says that when she entered in September 1947, her church was Lutheran. A year later in September 1948, she had her membership transferred from St. John's Lutheran in Des Moines to Hyde Park Presbyterian in Tampa. That information is typed at the bottom of her membership record from St. John's. We can only guess that she made the decision, in part, because Hyde Park was near where she lived. However, she may have been so upset and angry at Gruhn's behavior that she wanted to separate herself completely from the Lutheran church. Indeed, some women would simply have left the church entirely. I suspect Aunt Dot had faith and the church so deeply ingrained in her being that she was not ready to reject it entirely. However, in that era, theological beliefs and worship practices were distinct and different from one denomination to another. Some people's identities were tied to being Lutheran or Presbyterian or Episcopalian, etc. Non-denominational churches were virtually non-existent. We have no way of knowing what Aunt Dot told the clergy or staff at St. John's when she wrote and asked for a transfer of membership. Nor do we know if she told anyone in her family. What we do know for sure is that Aunt Dot was sufficiently focused and disciplined that she earned an A in Clinical Psychology and a B in Five Romantic Poets by the end of that fall term.

For the spring semester, she signed up for History of the United States and Contemporary Literature but withdrew from all classes on March 16, 1949. We do not know why. However, we know from her Hillsborough County School District application that she taught at the Day School for Partially Hearing from 1949 until she applied to teach in the public schools in 1951. Her salary increased from the previous $1,300 earned at Smith's school to $1,440 per year. It may be that the new load at the Day School became too much for her to manage along with the two university courses. It is also possible that she and

John Zambon had made plans to get married, and those arrangements entailed too much planning to do well in her two courses in addition.

We do not know when Aunt Dot met John, but my cousins and I are quite sure it occurred at the hospital. John served as a maintenance worker there, so it would have been easy, through casual contact, to get acquainted. I recall my father, Hub, saying once that Aunt Dot wanted Grandma and Grandpa to give her a wedding, but they refused. Hub offered no other information, and I didn't ask. Looking back and trying to piece together what happened, it seems probable that Aunt Dot may have gone home to Davenport in March 1949 to explain her plans to her parents. Her university transcript says that one copy of her record had been issued to herself at the Brady Street address in Davenport on March 8, 1949. Had she wanted her parents to see that she was very serious about going back to college and earning her degree? She probably thought Grandpa would be pleased with that progress. However, I believe that Aunt Dot had not told her parents all the details of Gruhn's behavior, and they probably still thought that being divorced was wrong. They may also have thought that marrying a man of Italian and Catholic background was not wise.

Nonetheless, Aunt Dot knew her own mind at this juncture in her life. She and John Anthony Zambon were married on July 9, 1949, by a judge at the courthouse in Tampa. Pictures in the Wagner family collection show John's sister, Rose, and his brother, Louis, as their attendants. Recently, Kimberly Tucker was able to locate Louis' widow, Lea Zambon. Now in her mid-90s, she confirmed that Aunt Dot and John had met at the hospital. She also told Kimberly how beautiful Aunt Dot's green wedding dress was. John's parents gave a wedding dinner for them. The newlyweds then moved into the apartment where Aunt Dot had been living on Davis Boulevard.

Getting married always requires many minor and major adjustments. Nonetheless, Aunt Dot maintained a Wagner pattern of keeping focused on long-term goals. She signed up for only one course for the fall term of 1949-1950, and completed that three-credit course on The Elementary Curriculum with a grade of B. At the same time, she continued teaching at the Day School. So she and John lived on her small teaching salary plus his wages from the hospital, since her alimony had ceased when she and John married.

We know virtually nothing about the Day School other than an article that appeared in *The Tampa Tribune* and also *The Tampa Times*, both on

Dot and John were married in Tampa in 1949.

Friday, November 19, 1949. The content suggests that a committed group of local citizens were working very hard to promote the best type of learning for children who were hearing impaired. The headline reads: "Open House Planned at School for Deaf at Drew Field Sunday." Hostesses for the open house were officers in the Society for the School of Deaf Children. Several names appear at the end of the article as hostesses. Included at the very end are faculty members: Mrs. Dorothea Morin, Mrs. Dorothy Zambon, and Mrs. W. P. Barrett. All interested people in the community were invited to attend the open house to see the facility, to "view the equipment that has been installed and to be told something of the work that is being done by the institution." From this article, it appears that Aunt Dot was one of three teachers, but Dorothea Morin also served as head of the school. She is one of the references Aunt Dot gave when she later applied to teach in the Hillsborough County School District.

For the spring semester of the 1949-50 academic year, Aunt Dot must have overestimated her time and energy when she signed up for two courses. She later withdrew from one of them but completed a four-credit course in Methods of Teaching Fine and Practical Arts, earning a grade of A. By the start of summer school, Aunt Dot had settled into married life and probably tried to make up for the previously dropped course. She signed up for four courses, totaling eleven credits. She earned two grades of B, one of B-, and one of C. John had to have been a supportive spouse for her to have completed her studies and, no doubt, kept up the house as well.

Entering what would be her final year of university work, Aunt Dot enrolled in three courses, totaling ten credits, for the fall term of 1950-1951. She earned three grades of B. Continuing with determination, she enrolled in four courses, plus chorus, for a total of thirteen credits during the spring semester of that year. She earned four grades of B and one of A. Finally, in summer school of 1951, Aunt Dot finished the last courses for her degree. Completing nine credits, she earned two grades of A and one of A-.

The summer term commencement exercises were announced in *The Tampa Times* on Friday, August 10, 1951. Dorothy Wagner Zambon's name appeared last among the alphabetically-listed graduates. However, she stood fourth academically in a class of thirty-four and was one of only nine women to receive a diploma. Aunt Dot graduated from the University of Tampa with a B.S. in Education—a major in Elementary Education and a minor in English. During the four years it had taken her to complete her degree, she had been deserted by her first husband, divorced him, married a second time, and learned, in addition to her university subjects, the specialized skills of teaching the deaf and hard-of-hearing child to speak. She was 38½ years old and finally ready for her own career.

Aunt Dot's forward progress contrasts dramatically with the choices that August Gruhn made during approximately the same time frame. She had started from nothing but being a loyal spouse and doing intermittent clerical work. Without women's support groups, without family support, and with little money, she had sacrificed and accomplished her goals over a four-year time period. Moreover, she had risked a second marriage with a man whose background was very different from hers and radically different from that of her first husband. Indeed, John Anthony Zambon was a Floridian of Italian and Catholic background, had not attended college, had served in the army as an enlisted man, and had never been married before. By contrast, a look at Gruhn's pattern of behavior, between the time he was discharged from the army and the early 1950s, highlights the resilience demonstrated by Aunt Dot in her progress toward a new life and suggests a personality profile that focused on himself and could easily have been abusive to Aunt Dot.

In the fall of 1947, when Aunt Dot entered the University of Tampa and continued her training at Sherman K. Smith's school, Gruhn was discharged from the army with the rank of Lieutenant Colonel, after completing his tour of duty as a supervising chaplain in the European Theater. He had finished his service in the army with a stellar record and, consequently, earned a good salary. Gruhn's choice of actions after his discharge from the army makes clear that, not only did he want out of his marriage, but he also did not want to return to the parish ministry. He would have known that, as a divorced minister, he would have appeared as a pariah to Lutherans sitting in the pews.

Moreover, going back to serve as pastor to a single congregation would have carried no glory compared to what he had experienced during the prior five years. He had enjoyed regular promotions—from Lieutenant to Captain to Major to Lieutenant Colonel. That meant a regular increase in status and salary. In addition, he had gone from an individual chaplain's work to becoming an instructor and supervisor. Serving as a supervisor in the China–Burma–India Theater and then in the European Theater from Rome to Cairo to Morocco meant foreign travel, publicity and wide, wide audiences. The entire experience would, no doubt, have made the Iowa Synod and St. John's Lutheran Church in Des Moines seem provincial, distant, and dull.

Tracing Gruhn's behavior, based on ELCA archival records,[37] requires looking ahead to the fall of 1950 when he applied for ecclesiastical endorsement to return to the chaplaincy. Even though Gruhn had served successfully during the war years, he still had to go through the same approval by church officials as had been required in 1942. His application is dated October 1, 1950. On October 2, Gynther Storaasli, in his role as Secretary for the Bureau of Service to Military Personnel, forwards Gruhn's application along with two others to Dr. C. E. Krumholz, then Secretary of the Army-Navy Committee of the ULCA.

On October 11, Gruhn writes to President Fred Boldt of the Iowa Synod, in effect, trying to get a favorable recommendation from him for a return to the military. Gruhn begins by telling Boldt that he finally has an upcoming interview, in his grade of Lieutenant Colonel, that could lead to getting back into the chaplaincy. He then explains why he had never attended synod meetings since his discharge from the army. A subsequent letter from President Boldt to Krumholz, dated October 21, 1950, says that when Gruhn left the chaplaincy, he called Boldt to say that he planned to go into some type of newspaper work. He also told Boldt that he would soon deposit his ordination papers with the synod. But Gruhn did not deposit the papers. Boldt says he knew nothing further about Gruhn's intentions until he received the above letter dated October 11, 1950, in which Gruhn alleges his wife's unfaithfulness and implies a subsequent divorce with Gruhn as the innocent party, as quoted here in chapter one. Thus, Gruhn had remained totally absent from the Iowa Synod for the preceding three years. Moreover, he had not stayed in regular contact with the president of the synod, despite Boldt saying he wrote to Gruhn several times to learn of his intentions. Nonetheless, the synod kept Gruhn on their clergy roster since, according to Boldt, "no action of any kind was taken or even contemplated without further information." Thus, despite his delinquent behavior, Gruhn continued as a "member of the Iowa Synod in good standing." Boldt closes his letter by telling Krumholz that he would be willing to give his endorsement to Gruhn's application for return to the chaplaincy.

---

[37] The ELCA file on Gruhn contains a sizeable collection of letters, some pictures, and some biographical data. The file contains nothing of his service record unless that information appears in letters to or from church officials.

Although veterans coming home after a lengthy stay abroad would have had difficulty adapting to civilian life, if Gruhn had really wanted to go back to a Lutheran pulpit, he could have talked with synod officials and developed a plan to achieve that goal. Similarly, if he had really wanted to stay in his marriage, he could have talked with Aunt Dot and employed a marriage counselor in order to develop skills necessary to restoring marital harmony. Given the limited grounds for divorce in Florida at that time, Gruhn had no legal basis on which to sue her for divorce. He could not prove her unfaithfulness. Thus, he had to concoct his lies about Aunt Dot's alleged adultery and then try to sell those lies to church officials when he tried in the fall of 1950 to return to the chaplaincy. One man bought into those lies.

Gynther Storaasli had been Gruhn's commanding officer for three years. He had brought Gruhn to San Antonio to be an instructor in the new Air Force Chaplains' School, and he had assigned Gruhn to CBI. Writing to Krumholz on October 2, Storaasli declared: "Throughout the three years he served under me, he did an outstanding job." Storaasli goes on to tell Krumholz that Gruhn lost two younger brothers during the war. One, a pilot, was lost on a bombing mission, and his body was never recovered. The other brother was a navigator who had been killed in England when his plane was returning from a mission. Storaasli then verifies that Gruhn had not been in active ministry since his discharge. "Cause? His first wife was unfaithful. He divorced her." Storaasli continues by saying that Gruhn was so upset over the situation that he "went into hiding as it were to recover his 'balance.'" He worked as a night clerk in a Washington, D.C. hotel. "After two years [sic] came out of his so-called seclusion, married again. Upon his statement of being the innocent party in his divorce, I performed his marriage."

On November 13, 1949, four months after Aunt Dot was remarried, Gruhn married a divorced woman of Catholic persuasion, who had a 15-year-old daughter. At Gruhn's request, Storaasli performed the ceremony. It took place in the Lutheran Church Center in Washington, D.C., according to public documents. Storaasli's letter of October 2 to Krumholz is not an endorsement of Gruhn, but appears to have been more of an explanation of Gruhn's status. Storaasli adds that, since coming out of his seclusion, "he has persistently sought to come back on active duty."

The Rev. Dr. Gynther Storaasli was no naïve, young chaplain. He was born in 1885, had been ordained in 1914, served as a missionary to China, and had also served as a parish pastor prior to entering the military chaplaincy program in World War I. During the World War II years, he had been the army's second Chief of Chaplains and had retired in 1948. Thus, he had served as a military chaplain for thirty years.[38] Having functioned in such varied capacities, domestic and foreign, commanding innumerable young chaplains, it is hard to believe that Gynther Storaasli was taken in by Gruhn's lies about Aunt Dot and his divorce. Two factors probably account for this. First, Storaasli liked Gruhn and thought he had proven to be an "outstanding" chaplain for the three years Storaasli had commanded Gruhn. Testimony to this record is the fact that Gruhn received fourteen times a rating of "Sup" in the army, according to his application for return to the chaplaincy. Perhaps even more important, the second reason probably accounting for Storaasli's being taken in by Gruhn's stories is that August Gruhn proved to be a consummate liar.

Although Boldt's endorsement was rather tepid, a very positive letter of recommendation, dated October 2? (print not clear), came to Krumholz from Gruhn's former colleague as associate pastor at St. John's Lutheran in Des Moines. Arthur Simonsen had received a request from Krumholz for a recommendation; his response is based only on pre-war work with Gruhn and some knowledge of his war record. Simonsen writes that Gruhn is "extremely capable, and I feel at the same time very sincere." Further, Simonsen writes that Gruhn's "personality is such that he is well-liked by the men in the service, and can perform a marvelous service among them." He closes his letter by "sincerely" recommending that Gruhn be endorsed for return to the chaplaincy.

Another former colleague is not so sure about Gruhn's qualifications and sincerity. Rev. Robert E. Van Deusen received an evaluation form from Paul C. Empie, Executive Secretary of the NLC, for a "candid opinion" as to the character of Gruhn at this time. Van Deusen's name had also been given as a reference by Gruhn. He states that he had known Gruhn when they both lived in Tampa during 1943-44. Van Deusen served as pastor at St. Paul Lutheran, and Gruhn served as chaplain at Drew Field. On several occasions, Gruhn spoke or preached in various programs at the church. According to Van Deusen, Gruhn had proved to be very successful with the military men during those war years. Now, in 1949-50, when Van Deusen knows Gruhn in the D.C. area, with no intervening contact, Van Deusen is not sure about Gruhn's qualifications for a return to the chaplaincy. Answering questions on the NLC form, Van

---

[38] Lawrence J. Lystig, "The Military Chaplaincy Program of the Evangelical Lutheran Church 1917 – 1960," (Master's Thesis, Luther Theological Seminary, 1977), chapter 4.

Deusen writes that he does not know if Gruhn's religious convictions are deeply rooted. Nor does he know if Gruhn has a "living Christian message." He further confirms that Gruhn is "out of active ministry at present." On a printed form where the scale is Poor, Medium, and Good, Van Deusen rates Gruhn as Medium for sense of humor, refinement, tact, and stability. He rates him as Good on voice, mental acumen, initiative, cooperativeness, liking for people, physical appearance, and executive ability. Van Deusen's narrative paragraph is even more telling:

> In Tampa, I considered him an excellent chaplain. Having renewed my acquaintance in a different setting, I am not quite so sure. Much depends on the appraisal of the interim when he was engaged in secular pursuits. His explanation is that he wanted to spare the church the embarrassment of his domestic troubles, ending in divorce. If that is true and he is trying to make a comeback, I should like to see him have his chance. To be quite honest, however, my impression of him at this time is not so favorable as it was in Tampa, *I am not quite sure of his bedrock sincerity* (italics mine).

Van Deusen concludes by recommending Gruhn with "reservations." At that time, Van Deusen served as Washington Secretary, Division of Public Relations for the NLC.

With the endorsements, as noted above, Gruhn's application moves through channels. On November 10, 1950, Krumholz signs the official "Endorsement—Chaplaincy Application U.S. Army—Active Duty." On November 17, the official endorsement goes to the Office of Chief of Chaplains. Storaasli has learned of this endorsement and writes a letter of protest to Paul C. Empie, Executive Director of the NLC. Storaasli says that he was "greatly surprised" at the endorsement and he disagrees with it. He has only one ground for disagreeing with the action, namely that Gruhn was not engaged in active ministry and had not been since his discharge from the military. Regulations for men to enter the chaplaincy had always stipulated that the candidate be serving in the capacity of his calling or in some related capacity in the church.

Several months later, Storaasli receives a letter from Major General Roy N. Parker, Chief of Chaplains, dated July 6, 1951, asking Storaasli to explain Gruhn's status in relation to the church. "On his application, Chaplain Gruhn indicates that from 1947 to the present he has been self-employed as a writer, and employed as editor of correspondence with indefinite assignment, for the United Lutheran Church." Parker goes on, basically, to reiterate Storaasli's point about regulations for those wanting to enter the chaplaincy. "All applicants . . . must be actively engaged in the ministry as their principal vocation in life, or must hold a position with the church, or must be engaged in duties which have the approbation of the church." Three days later, Storaasli writes the then-president of the Committee on Army and Navy Work. He asks Rev. Robert Lee to look into the matter which Parker raised.

On August 20, Paul C. Empie writes Gruhn that the NLC is withdrawing their endorsement of him for return to the chaplaincy. "This action has been taken according to the regular procedures established by which the council acts as the agency for its participating bodies." All parties involved in the process are notified of the withdrawal of endorsement.

On August 31 Storaasli writes Gruhn a pastoral letter. He empathizes with Gruhn's disappointment, but then speaks to the biblical and conscience issue involved. "I have for a long time since meeting you again in Washington been laboring under the impression that you have somehow allowed your own cause as an ordained minister [to] become confused with that of God's cause." He goes on to stress that once a man is called and accepted into the "Holy Ministry," he cannot then do as he pleases. Storaasli is clearly a man of firm Christian character and conscience; thus, he encourages Gruhn to look deep into his own soul and think about his choices. Gruhn, it appears, chose to follow his own desires.

His file in the ELCA archive includes an envelope with typed address: Office of the Secretary, The United Lutheran Church in America, 231 Madison Avenue, New York 16, New York USA. Handwritten on the envelope is the following:

> Mr. Gruhn has been employed, since he left the chaplaincy on night desk in Hamilton Hotel, and at Chevy Chase Country Club, Wash. D.C., and has run a meat business in a Wash. D.C. market. This info given [words not clear] 9-1-53 by Chaplain Storaasli.

Also included in Gruhn's file is a copy of his roll card as a member of the Iowa Synod, dated 6/20/53. Typed on the card is "Deposit of ordination papers, Jan. 30, 1953." Hand written is a note that says "Stays on the roll!"

On September 22, 1953, the then Secretary of the ULCA, F. Eppling Reinartz, writes Storaasli to say that Gruhn remained on the roll of ministers for the ULCA and the Iowa Synod. According to Reinartz, correspondence indicates that the Iowa Synod did not consider Gruhn's present business "incompatible with the nature of the Office of the Holy Ministry." When reading this letter, Storaasli explodes. The next day, he writes Reinartz and says that he could say much about the position of the Iowa Synod, but allows that it had better be left unsaid. "But I cannot refrain from asking what compatibility is there between the job of night hotel clerk in a second-rate hotel, running a meat counter in a market on the side, and the Holy Ministry?" Gruhn continued in his secular occupations, and was not removed from the clergy rolls until 1956.

During all of this correspondence, including lies and failed attempts to return to the chaplaincy, Gruhn had been married to his second wife, whose teenage daughter had been living with them. Through a public records search and some good luck, Kimberly Tucker was able to get in contact with this daughter, now an older woman, whose name will not be used in order to protect her privacy. The woman permitted Kimberly to record their phone conversations; she has also signed a permission form to use the following contents in this story.

In a radical departure from his first marriage to Aunt Dot, Gruhn and his second wife appear to have had little in common. She was five years older than he. She had been born in Europe and survived the ravages of World War I but with some serious health issues. Her daughter told Kimberly that her mother suffered from extremely high blood pressure and very painful tension headaches. Mother and daughter had emigrated to America when the daughter was 3 years old. Living in Washington, D.C., the mother apparently made a living by cooking, being employed at some celebrated restaurants.

The daughter recalled that Gruhn ran some kind of a correspondence school or newspaper office, but he didn't make much money. The three of them lived in a one-bedroom apartment; the daughter had to do her homework in the living room and sleep on a couch in that room. She resented Gruhn intruding into her private space at night when she was trying to study and listen to her ballet music. In particular, she resented his conversations turning to questions about her boyfriends and to sex. She felt that was abusive. In addition, she told about one occasion when her mother was out of town and Gruhn took her to a major league ball game, since she was a fan of one of the players. After the game they went to a hotel restaurant and Gruhn bought her liquor. She admits that she was trying to be sophisticated, but was truly naïve. The ultimate result was that when they got back to their apartment, she was "drunk as a skunk."

Elaborating on the difficulties of little money in the household, the daughter said that she got a job at the FBI when she was 19 or 20, and she had to give all her paychecks over to support the family. In fact, she thinks that, if she hadn't gone to work, they wouldn't have made it at all. Part of the time, her mother was simply very ill and had surgery that prevented her from working. Thus, Gruhn was not supporting his family. The daughter left home eventually, just to get away from him. Sadly, her early marriage turned out to also be an abusive situation. About the time that Gruhn was removed from clergy rolls, the second wife left Gruhn and moved west. Subsequently, she began getting phone calls from debt collectors who said she owed this and that. All were expenses that Gruhn had incurred, but he was trying to stick his wife with the charges.

Ultimately, Gruhn sued his second wife for desertion, according to Florida marriage records, and married a third time within two weeks of the divorce, to a woman two decades younger than he was.

Again, by searching public records, coupled with good fortune, Kimberly Tucker was able to speak with Gruhn's third wife and, with permission, to record the conversation. She also signed a permission slip to use the contents of their conversation in this story.

The wife said that Gruhn claimed he left the chaplaincy because Aunt Dot had threatened to ruin him with the church if he divorced her. Further, he told this third wife that Aunt Dot had an affair when he was overseas, got pregnant, and had an abortion. He declared that if Aunt Dot had not had an abortion, he would have stayed in the marriage with her. A further lie appears on their marriage license; Gruhn gave his age as 40, when it was actually 50.

Thus, following his discharge from the army, Gruhn's choices and behavior resulted in a downward spiral from his days of glory in the chaplaincy corps. Not only did he discard Aunt Dot, but he also discarded his vocation as an ordained minister of the gospel and apparently turned his back on the church.

In contrast, the remainder of Aunt Dot's short life involved her new teaching career and a second marriage that my cousins and I thought appeared to be smooth and harmonious for both individuals. However, as sometimes happens when one investigates a family's history, some surprises appear.

Notes

- Kimberly's good fortune in connecting with Mr. James Short is due to the fact that she had posted Mary Bach's family tree online. Mr. Short saw it, was very interested in hearing more about his former teacher, and so contacted Kimberly.

- August Gruhn and his third wife had a long and, apparently, satisfying marriage. Ultimately, he reinvented himself. His third wife shared copies of letters and a biographical sketch, which indicate that Gruhn became successful in the hotel management industry. According to public documents, he lived a long life and is buried in Arlington National Cemetery.

- August Gruhn's second wife lived a long life despite her health issues. Her daughter divorced her abusive husband and married a second time to a man whom she describes as almost saintly.

John Zambon's brother, Louis, and sister, Rose, served as best man and maid of honor.

CHAPTER EIGHT

A Second Marriage with a Surprise Twist

My cousins and I knew Aunt Dot's second husband, John Zambon, only during brief summer visits when the two came to Davenport to visit our grandparents or to Plainfield, Iowa, visiting Gene and family. John appeared to be a personable man, easy to get along with. And he seemed to love children. Cousin Nancy retains one fond memory of a summer visit to Lake Okiboji in Iowa, probably in 1950, when both families were present, including Grandma and Grandpa. Nancy recalls that she did not like getting sand in her feet. So John would carry her from the edge of the water to the grassy area. Caroline would say, "Oh, John, you don't have to do that!" Obviously, he wanted to. In the family picture taken at the time of our grandparents' fiftieth wedding anniversary, Nancy is sitting cozily next to John, as is older brother, Tom. When cousin Pam was born in February 1954, pictures show both Aunt Dot and John holding the baby, smiling and delighting in her six-month-old expressions and movements.

Before John married into the Wagner family in July 1949, he had grown up in Tampa and graduated from high school there. He came from a modest background; his parents had emigrated from Sicily in the early part of the twentieth century. John's father, Salvator Zambon, was trained as a shoemaker and ran his own shop; his mother ran the household. John was the oldest, born in 1915. He was followed by Louis and Rose, within four years. John's mother, Sara DiLorenzo Zambon, also had a brother and sister living in the neighborhood—Anthony DiLorenzo and Mary DiLorenzo Puleo. Their families were three of many immigrant households residing in the section of Tampa known as Ybor City, where the Italian Club served as a social and business gathering spot.

Although Aunt Dot had grown up in a family where Grandpa had set aside money from the beginning for his children to go to college, John's background was very different. He graduated from Hillsborough High

School in 1936, at age 21, and then worked for a company in the production of beverages. It was unskilled work. Why the delay in finishing high school, we do not know. However, we cousins knew at once when we met John that he had a vision problem in one eye. Cousin Nancy remembers that Gene said it was probably due to some kind of disease. Although John had virtually no vision in that eye, he still served in the army, though not in combat.

According to World War II army enlistment files, John A. Zambon enlisted on August 18, 1942, at Camp Blanding, Florida, and served in the Branch Immaterial—Warrant Officers, USA. His enlistment was for the duration of the war or other emergency, plus six months, "subject to the discretion of the President or otherwise according to law." At the time of enlistment, John had been living at his parents' home, stood sixty-nine inches tall and weighed 136 pounds.

Serving in the grade structure known as Warrant Officers meant that John had received special training in technical fields such as medical, ordinance, mechanical, or some other. These were not combat fields but required specialized training. Due to the fire at the National Personnel Records Center in St. Louis, we have no information about where John served, except we know that his four years of army service were in this country. His final pay voucher says that he was honorably discharged on March 14, 1946, at Fort McPherson in Georgia. The dollar balance due him amounted to $158.89. The U.S. Veterans Gravesites record identifies John's final ranking as "TEC 5 US Army World War II."

When John came home from army service, he again lived at his parents' home in Ybor City. At some point, he got a job as a maintenance worker at Tampa Municipal Hospital, where Aunt Dot had been working as a clerk. We have no knowledge of when in time she and John met or when they began dating. It certainly would have been after October 1946, since that was the time when Gruhn came home and told Aunt Dot that he would never again live with her. During 1947, she was recovering her equilibrium, preparing for a divorce, learning to teach hearing-impaired children, returning to college, and working part-time to support herself. During the same period, John would have needed time and space to adjust to civilian life after four years in the army. It seems likely that Aunt Dot and John would not have dated seriously until after her divorce was final in early March 1948. They both would have required time and space to readjust their personal priorities in the new peacetime society.

Choosing a spouse when one is older, and wounded like Aunt Dot had been, requires careful thought to see if the relationship will actually work. Certainly, John Zambon was about as opposite as one could get from August Gruhn. However, that reality may have appealed to Aunt Dot. According to city directories, they lived in Aunt Dot's apartment on Davis Boulevard from the time they were married until late 1955, when they bought a house. That was six years in a small apartment when Aunt Dot was also taking classes at the university and teaching part-time until she finished her bachelor's degree and was hired full-time. That kind of permanence in living situation contrasted with her annual moves in Des Moines and then trailing all over the country trying to be near Gruhn when he was in the army.

Living in close quarters when both spouses are working and studying certainly requires give and take as well as careful time and money management. Additional insight into the marriage relationship comes from John's nephew, Sam Zambon, who lives in Tampa. The son of Louis Zambon, John's brother, Sam told us that he had enjoyed some extended conversations with his uncle when John was in the last years of his life. In recorded conversations with us, Sam said that John called Aunt Dot, "Dottie." He "definitely loved her big time" and liked to reminisce about her. She was "good natured," "loved kids," liked to read, and was a member of a local Lutheran church. Aunt Dot and John also enjoyed some common interests. According to Sam, they had parties and dressed up for Halloween trick or treaters. They also shared a love of opera and going out to dinner. And they went weekly to family dinners at Salvator and Sara's house. John knew that Aunt Dot couldn't have children, but that didn't bother him. Sam said that John was also very proud of Aunt Dot being a school teacher.

In addition, Aunt Dot gained a sister in Rose Zambon. The two women each had older brothers but no sisters, so the relationship must have been good for both of them. Sam said that it was an Italian custom for children to live in the parental home until they got married. In the case of his Aunt Rose, he thought perhaps that Salvator, Rose's father, might have scared off any potential suitors. Rose lived with her parents all of her life and helped them in their later years. She also had a responsible job as office manager of the Hillsborough County motor vehicle department. I recall that one summer, when Aunt Dot and John made their annual trip north to visit the Wagners, Rose came with them. They all stayed in Grandpa and Grandma's two-bedroom, upstairs apartment, which had only one bathroom. So they must have gotten along in an amiable and respectful fashion. I remember Hub remarking once that "Dot really likes Rose."

Although John did not have a college degree, we cannot conclude that he, therefore, lacked the abilities for successful higher education. John may not have wanted to continue study beyond high school. That tradition did not exist in his family. Moreover, John's lack of sight in one eye may have been a serious deterrent. However, Sam said that John spoke three languages—English, Spanish, and Italian. Sam also noted that John was a skilled locksmith, and he was trained as a technician in the army. Sam thought he had served as a medic, though not on the battlefield. Further, Sam added that his uncle was ambidextrous when it came to writing. Thus, John possessed manual skills and a mind that worked accordingly.

Additional insight comes from an article in *The Tampa Tribune* for December 4, 1949. John and another man are pictured in front of a very large crate, below the headline: "Big Massage Tank Arrives for Polio Ward." The two men are dwarfed by the wooden crate. In an era when polio was rampant in the country, citizens of Tampa had contributed money for the hospital to buy the "latest and costliest piece of equipment." For $3,800, the hydromassage therapy tank permitted "full body immersion." The new tank replaced an old bath tub which required two nurses to lift a patient in and out plus agitate the water by hand. John and the other man are identified as "hospital maintenance men." Clearly, John's work at the hospital involved keeping all kinds of machinery in good working order.

Concrete evidence of the fact that John really loved and respected Aunt Dot seems self-evident from the fact that she completed the last two years of courses for her degree when they were newly married and living in her small apartment. Without a college degree of his own, John must have had a very strong ego to support his wife in her accomplishments toward a teaching career, given that the era was one in which men still ruled the world of power, money, and upward mobility. Although women had filled men's jobs during the war, when the veterans came home, they had priority. Women were expected to give up their jobs. Men were still considered the breadwinners and women the housewives. Although Aunt Dot had fulfilled that role in her marriage to Gruhn, she and John certainly had an understanding such that he respected and supported her determination to finish her degree and teach.

Moreover, early on in their marriage John began coming north with Aunt Dot to take their annual vacations in Iowa. They probably first travelled to Davenport in the summer of 1950. Aunt Dot had carried eleven credits during the summer school session. A trip north in August might have been a welcome break for her. However, in 1951, when Grandma and Grandpa celebrated their fiftieth wedding anniversary, we know for sure that Aunt Dot and John joined Hardt, Hub, Gene, their wives, and children to honor their parents. The picture of everyone sitting on the front steps of the Brady Street house in Davenport testifies to the fact that John seemed especially well liked by cousins Nancy and Tom. The gathering probably happened in August, after Aunt Dot had gone through commencement exercises at the University of Tampa. But in the spring of 1951, she had already applied to the Hillsborough County School District for a teaching position.

We have Aunt Dot's public employment record with Hillsborough County and also her Teacher's Permanent Record Card. These documents give statements of reference from the people she had studied and worked under while preparing to teach full-time. They further testify to Aunt Dot's determination to begin her own career as a teacher.

On her application to teach in HCSD, dated May 17, 1951, she wrote:

> My Educational Philosophy—Education for elementary age children is a challenge to the highest and best in all who associate themselves with this work. A love of children is the prime requisite when one considers teaching the very young child. Children have always interested me and I feel a great satisfaction in being a part of the formulation of the characters of the children who will be the future voting citizens of the U.S. I have been particularly interested in the handicapped child and want to give the best I know to that child who needs additional help in preparation for meeting the demands which will be placed upon him in a democratic society.

Her thoughts are further corroborated by subsequent statements where she says that she intended to continue her study and earn a master's degree, perhaps even a Ph.D. Clearly, she knew she had the ability for graduate work, and she possessed the drive that had characterized her older brothers, who all attained advanced degrees.

Among the references she cited, Aunt Dot named Sherman K. Smith. Specifically she wrote, "I received training from Dr. Smith in the mechanics of speech, the physiology and anatomy of the speech organs, and phonetics, though I did not receive college credit for this training." On a scale of "outstanding, superior, good, satisfactory, poor, failure," Smith gave Aunt Dot a "satisfactory" rating but amplified his evaluation. He stated that he would employ Aunt Dot if he had a supervising teacher to direct her work. He noted that acquiring the teaching skills needed for this highly specialized field required a very long time. Hence, he wrote that "Mrs. Zambon would do good to work under supervision of a teacher with years of experience." He further noted that he had known Aunt Dot for about five years "as a teacher and as a pupil."

Writing with a different perspective, Dr. Dorothea W. Morin, Principal of the Day School for Partially Hearing, recognized Aunt Dot's load in teaching part-time and attending the university part-time. She wrote:

> Mrs. Zambon is a hard worker—has carried a tremendous load between teaching in a most difficult and trying situation, and has also taken a number of courses and [earned?] her degree at the University of Tampa at the same time. I believe her to be very capable, conscientious, well-balanced, (and) intelligent. Besides that, she is interested in working for exceptional children, and willing to take the additional work (necessary or required) for certification in this field.

A still different perspective comes from the evaluation of Aunt Dot by Dr. Zoe Cowen, head of the Elementary Education Department at the University of Tampa. Dr. Cowen stated that she would employ Aunt Dot and ranked her as "superior" on the same scale that Smith used. Thus, all three references considered Aunt Dot to have ability, and the two women gave her a superlative rating. Aunt Dot went on to teach in the Hillsborough County School District from 1951 to 1961.

We know about her teaching assignments from her Teacher's Permanent Record Card and newspaper accounts. In *The Tampa Times* for August 28, 1951, in an article listing new teacher assignments in the school district, Aunt Dot was assigned to Bayside School. She taught there from the fall of 1951 through the spring semester of 1954. For each of those years, her Permanent Record Card says that she taught the "hard of hearing."

An article in *The Times* for November 15, 1951, tells more about the school, even though the headline reads: "Bayside PTA Schedules Annual Silver Tea Tomorrow." After citing all the women helping with the tea, the reporter pointed out some distinctive information about Bayside School. It had only existed since 1946 when the County's Society for Crippled Children and Adults had organized the school. It was the "first of its kind in this section of the state and was incorporated into the Florida educational system by the law of 1947." In November 1951, the school had "56 orthopedically handicapped or hard of hearing children" enrolled. Further, the reporter noted, "Bayside is now recognized all over the country as one of the out-standing examples in education for the exceptional child." The tea served as a fund-raiser to supply equipment beyond what the department of education had funded.

Another group, called the Bayshore Garden Circle, also helped raise funds for Bayside School. *The Tampa Times* for Sunday, March 8, 1953, shows Aunt Dot and several children using the Train-Ear. At least six children, comprising a class for "deaf and hard of hearing," are shown with ear phones. "Standing are Mrs. John Zambon, teacher (left), and Mrs. Elton Edwards, garden therapy chairman for the fifth district of Florida."

For the 1954-55 school year, Aunt Dot was transferred to the V. M. Ybor School where she continued for the next six years. Community interest in helping the hearing-impaired child apparently remained strong in Tampa. *The Tampa Times* for August 29, 1955, carried a picture of Aunt Dot, a student, and two adults from the community. The headline reads: "Pilot Club Presents Hearing Trainer." Members of the Local Pilot International baked and sold fruit cakes to raise money for a machine called "Maico Train-Ear." It is being used in the V.M. Ybor School, with Miss [sic] Dorothy Zambon as teacher" under the supervision of the Director of Special Education. The unique features of this machine included headphones and separate volume controls for each ear:

> The one machine will take care of ten pupils, and will reach the most severely deafened; it has been able to reach hearing in children where both the Audiometer and hearing aids have failed, as it can vary its tones to stress "highs" or "lows" to fit the output to the individual.

The next year, Aunt Dot is again pictured with students using the Train-Ear. This photo appeared in *The Times* for March 14, 1956, and identifies the students as from a "Special classroom for hard-of-hearing at V. M. Ybor School." The machine had been provided by "one of women's classified service clubs." Again in *The Times* for May 27, 1958, Aunt Dot is pictured receiving a check from women representing the

A Second Marriage with a Surprise Twist | 143

local chapter of Sigma Alpha Iota National Music Fraternity. Records and "special equipment" were to be purchased with the money received.

In addition to finally being engaged in her own career, Aunt Dot also came to enjoy what was, no doubt, a longed-for acquisition—her own home. According to *The Tampa Times* for November 17, 1955, in a listing of real estate transactions, Aunt Dot and John paid $12,100 to Tam-Ami Homes, Inc. for their new home. Property records indicate that 4421 Fairoaks Avenue was part of a development known as Guernsey Estates. Driving by that address today, we see modest homes, probably dating from the post-WWII housing boom. Aunt Dot would have enjoyed a two-bedroom home, and John would have had a small yard to take care of. John told Sam that they paid cash for the house and had no mortgage. Property records confirm there was no mortgage and that aggregate taxes for 1956 amounted to $114.76.

Not having a mortgage suggests that they had been able to save money for the previous four years when Aunt Dot had been earning a full-time salary. Although the price of $12,100 sounds cheap in today's terms, salaries were equally modest by today's standards. An article in *The Tampa Times* for February 28, 1953, gives perspective on teachers' pay. The headline capsuled the story: "Solid Front Asked On Teacher Pay Hike." Over 500 members of the Hillsborough County Education Association had gathered the previous night for a two-hour session in the Tampa Terrace Hotel. The purpose was to hear "a panel discussion by educators, legislators and a representative of the Florida Citizens' Committee on Education talk on problems facing the state's growing school system." In effect, the state school superintendent was pleading with teachers to get together on how much of a salary increase they wanted from the state legislature. Superintendent Bailey presented a graph showing that Hillsborough County's teachers received the third highest average salaries among Florida's counties. In dollar figures, the county's teachers commanded average salaries of "approximately $3,450" per year. That total was $235.31 above the state average. That annual salary was also "above the national average."

Chances are that Aunt Dot received a salary below the average since she only had two years of experience in the school system. On the other hand, she might have commanded higher pay for a more specialized position. Nonetheless, by November 1955 when she and John bought their house, she had only been able to save money for the previous four years. Moreover, she may have had some debts to pay from the prior

On the left, Tom, Kate, and Nancy, children of Gene and Caroline, with John holding Pam and Dot looking on. On the right, Dot enjoying her niece, Pam, daughter of Gene and Caroline. Both photos were taken summer 1954 in the yard of the Plainfield house where Gene had his office as the doctor.

In undated photo, Dot and John in Florida.

Dot and John, in an undated photo, together in Florida.

Aunt Dot's Zambon Family Connections

Santo Trafficante, Sr.
b. 1886 in Sicily

SONS
Frank, b. abt. 1911
Santo, Jr. "The Silent Don," b. 1914
Sam, b. 1916
Fano, husband of "Angie," b. 1919
Pallbearer for Aunt Dot
Henry, b. abt. 1925

Salvator Zambon
b. 1885 in Sicily

SONS
John Anthony, b. 1915
Husband of Aunt Dot
Louis A., b. 1917
DAUGHTER
Rosa "Rose," b. 1919
GRANDSON
Sam, b. 1959

DILORENZO SIBLINGS

Sara DiLorenzo **Zambon**, b. 1896 in Italy
Wife of Salvator, Mother of John Zambon

Anthony "Tony" DiLorenzo, b. 1904
Uncle of John Zambon
Father of John A. DiLorenzo
Testified in Kefauver Hearings

John A. DiLorenzo, b. 1940
Pallbearer for Aunt Dot

Mary DiLorenzo Puleo, b. 1907
Aunt of John Zambon
Mother of Angelina "Angie" Puleo Trafficante

years when she really had had to scrape by. It was not possible to get information on salaries for maintenance men working at Tampa Municipal Hospital. But we can assume that his position paid less than Aunt Dot's salary. Thus, it seems unlikely that they would have been able to save $12,100 in four years time, given that they would also have had extra expenses with moving and furnishing a full house. Perhaps they received help from family; we will never know for sure.

Just when Aunt Dot seemed to have achieved a loving marriage and a satisfying teaching career, fate reared an ugly head. According to her death certificate, she was diagnosed with breast cancer in February 1957. Little was known about cancer at that time, compared with today. Mammography was not refined and used until the 1960s. Annual breast checks were not advocated by physicians. Chances are that Aunt Dot happened to notice a lump in her breast in some happenstance fashion. My cousins and I know that she underwent, at some future date, a radical mastectomy. We can remember her wearing an elastic sleeve to keep the swelling down in her arm. Undoubtedly, some lymph nodes and/or muscle tissue had been removed, and that necessitated the sleeve. Then on Father's Day, in June 1958, Grandpa died suddenly but peacefully from a heart attack. Cousin Nancy and I do not recall Aunt Dot coming home to Davenport for the funeral. She may have had her surgery about that time and/or been undergoing additional treatment. What we do know for sure is that Aunt Dot did not let cancer or her father's death paralyze her.

She continued to teach at the V. M. Ybor School through 1960. For the 1960-61 school year, she was moved to Foster School. We do not know for sure if she finished out the second semester. Her death certificate says that she died on June 24, 1961, in the hospital. The certificate does not say when she was hospitalized. Cause of death was carcinoma of the left breast with metastasis to the spine and pelvis. That would have left her in serious pain at some point in the journey from diagnosis to death. She would have been given pain medication, probably also radiation, but likely nothing else was able to be done for her.

Gene flew to Tampa for the funeral. Hub and Olive drove down from Rock Island. Upon returning from the funeral, Hub remarked about the large number of people who came, either to the visitation or funeral. Nancy recalls Gene telling that he had talked with one of Aunt Dot's former students. The young woman spoke in a normal tone of voice. In fact, he did not know that she had been one of Aunt Dot's students until the woman told him. Enabling the hard-of-hearing and deaf child to speak in a normal voice tone had always been the goal of Sherman K. Smith when he opened his school and was teaching Aunt Dot.

John was devastated by her death. Nancy recalls that later in the summer John packed up Aunt Dot's possessions which belonged to the Wagner family and drove north. Included among those possessions was a set of Bavarian china with twelve-place settings and several serving dishes. John brought this well-packed china to Gene's family in Plainfield. According to Nancy, John was very distraught, telling Gene that he drove fast and didn't care if he crashed or not. Gene was so concerned with this state of mind that he persuaded John to stay over an extra couple of days so that the two could talk, and John would, hopefully, be able to drive safely back to Tampa.

We cousins did not see John again, but we know that he married in 1962. Public records show that the marriage lasted only a year and ended in divorce. His third wife outlived John, who died in 2004 at age 89. But the marriage was apparently not successful. According to Sam, Aunt Dot was really his only true love.

It was not long after Kimberly had sent me the newspaper accounts of Aunt Dot's death and funeral that she called me excitedly one morning with the following announcement: **"Ann, Ann, the pallbearers for Aunt Dot have mafia family names!"** I was as shocked as I had been when first reading Gruhn's allegations about Aunt Dot's behavior (chapter one).

Had my aunt forsaken her Lutheran background and become mixed up in an underworld family? To those of us living in the Midwest, outside of Chicago, the name "mafia" conjures up images of the movie, *The Godfather*, and organized crime. When reading the newspaper clipping on Aunt Dot's death and funeral, I had seen the same names of pallbearers that Kimberly had seen. But I knew nothing about mafia in Tampa, so all I could see was that the names appeared to be Italian. As a long-time resident of Tampa and one who had read about mafia history in the city, Kimberly recognized the significance of the names. Trying to sort out any possible mafia connections with John, and then trying to figure out what Aunt Dot knew and when she knew it, has been a focus for months of research, careful thought, and analysis.

Thanks to Kimberly's digging into the Zambon, DiLorenzo, and Puleo families, it is clear that the pallbearers for Aunt Dot were John's cousins on his mother's side. Some were cousins by marriage and one by blood. John A. DiLorenzo was the son of Sara Zambon's younger brother, Anthony or "Tony" DiLorenzo. Sara's younger sister, Mary DiLorenzo Puleo, had only daughters. Thus, another pallbearer, Fano Trafficante, married one of those daughters, Angelina Puleo, and became John's cousin by marriage. Additional pallbearers married other Puleo daughters, hence were also cousins to John by marriage. Of the six pallbearers, the two names which leaped out to Kimberly were John A. DiLorenzo and Fano Trafficante. In order to make any sense of their relationships with John and Aunt Dot, we have to do a brief trip through the recorded history of mafia in Tampa.

Author and researcher, Scott M. Deitche has written two books on the subject. *Cigar City Mafia: A Complete History of the Tampa Underworld*, which came out in 2004. *The Silent Don: The Criminal Underworld of Santo Trafficante Jr.* was published in 2009. Focused on the Trafficante family, this latter book serves our present purpose.

Santo Trafficante Sr. was born within one year of Salvator Zambon, John's father. Both had emigrated to this country from Sicily in the early twentieth century and settled in the Ybor City section of Tampa, where family and ethnic ties remained close over decades. Like their respective fathers, Santo Jr. and John Zambon were the oldest in their families and born within one year of each other. Both also later went to Hillsborough High School. Unlike John Zambon, who graduated from high school, Santo Jr. dropped out at about age 16.

Deitche writes that it is not clear just when Santo Sr. became involved with organized mafia crime activity. But by the late 1920s, he "was recognized by underworld leaders in other areas of the country as one of the dominant mob figures in Tampa. His power was closely tied into relationships with New York crime figures." However, there were other authority figures to deal with in Tampa. Santo Sr. carefully consolidated his power so that when he died in 1954, Santo Jr. was ready to assume the mantle of boss. The father had slowly groomed the son, recognizing the young man's aptitude for the role he was to assume. Although Santo Jr. had four brothers, Frank, the oldest, had "little affinity for the rackets." Henry and Sam concentrated "on their own respective illegal gambling empires." Like older brother Frank, Fano "had little overt interest in the crime family management." For Santo Jr. the management eventually extended over an empire that ultimately stretched from Tampa to Havana to Europe and to the Far East.[39]

---

[39] Scott M. Deitche, *The Silent Don: The Criminal Underworld of Santo Trafficante, Jr.* (Fort Lee, New Jersey: Barricade Books, Inc., 2009), 8, 16, 23-4, 56.

As I wondered what Aunt Dot knew of this Trafficante family, I asked Kimberly to find all the newspaper stories about them from the 1950s that were available digitally. Aunt Dot would have regularly read the daily newspapers. Perhaps the most notorious story of these resurrected accounts involved the death of John's cousin, Angelina Puleo Trafficante. The column headline from *The Tampa Times* for March 17, 1953, reads: "Hospital Patient Jumps to Death." The opening paragraph reports the core of the story: "A 26-year-old Tampa woman plunged to her death from a sixth floor Municipal Hospital window yesterday afternoon, shortly after a nurse's aide combed her hair and reported the patient was in 'fine spirits.'" Angie had been admitted to the hospital the previous Friday; her death was called a suicide. The part of the story that is very difficult to believe is that investigating officers said she "apparently used a burst of super-human strength to wrench loose several horizontal bars on a bathroom window that were secured with four-inch bolts." In addition to the nurse's aide who combed Angie's hair, two other attendants "reported the woman was in a good frame of mind just prior to the incident." The article closes by identifying Angie's husband, Fano Trafficante, as operator of the Flamingo Bar and Lounge. Besides her husband, Angie was survived by a son, Santo Jose, born in January.

The Times for March 18 carried the funeral notice. It was set for 4:00 p.m. that day. Fano's brothers, Frank, Sam, and Henry Trafficante, served as pallbearers, as did two of Angie's brothers-in-law and John Zambon.

Three months later, *The Tampa Tribune* for June 25, carried an article headed by: "Husband Sues City in Death Leap of Wife from Hospital." Fano had filed a suit against the city for $250,000, alleging that hospital officials and attendants had been careless and negligent in the care of Angie. It was further stated that she had made two "unsuccessful attempts to commit suicide" before her death. Two years later, *The Tribune* carried a story on June 23, 1955, which reported that the city had finally paid Fano $7,500 in damages. Before the final jury verdict, he had filed an amended complaint, asking only $100,000 in damages.

According to Kimberly's research and Sam Zambon's knowledge, the case was never really solved. Young married women in 1953 did not engage in weight training to build muscle that would have allowed her to pry open the window bars. Moreover, she had just given birth two months before her death. We can only speculate on what John thought, what Aunt Dot might have asked him about his cousin, and how he responded.

Another published link between John's family and the mafia is the transcript of Anthony "Tony" DiLorenzo being interviewed by a member of the United States Senate's Kefauver Committee. Long before Watergate, even before the Army-McCarthy hearings, those conducted by the Senate Committee to Investigate Crime and Interstate Commerce became front-page print news and widely watched television news. Initiated by Tennessee Senator Estes Kefauver, these hearings were held in major cities around the country. They came to Tampa in late 1950. In sworn testimony comprising about twenty pages of transcript, John's uncle was asked questions, to which he regularly gave evasive answers. In another several pages of testimony, Anthony DiLorenzo's wife was asked about his guns. In one response, she said that he kept some guns at his house and some at the home of his brother-in-law, Salvator Zambon.[40]

Further insight on the guns came from John's nephew, Sam Zambon. In one conversation, he said that when he was about 13 or 14, John had given him a Derringer that Sam's great-uncle "Tony" had originally given to John. According to Sam, "They were really big into hiding guns in the houses." Both at his parents' house and his grandfather's house, there were all kinds of hidden compartments—built into walls or furniture or floorboards in closets—where guns could be stashed.

Sam told us one other story which suggests that the Zambons were somehow connected to the mafia. He said that when he told John that he was going to get married, John gave Sam a ring to give to his fiancé. It had originally belonged to Salvator. The ring had a full-carat flawless stone, of European cut. In Sam's words: "My grandfather was a shoemaker. He had a store off and on and also he worked for the school board for a time at Ybor Elementary. Why would a shoemaker have a ring like this?"

By Sam's own account, his father Louis had protected him from the mafia family. Sam knew nothing about any mafia connections until later in his life when he started piecing together incidents, like the story about the ring. He also remembered that when he was a young boy and would go with his parents to large social or political gatherings, men would come up to Salvator and give him a kiss on the cheek or on his hand as

---

[40] Investigation of Organized Crime in Interstate Commerce, Hearings Before a Special Committee, United States Senate 81st Congress Second Session and 82nd Congress First Session, Pursuant to Senate Resolution 202 (81st Congress). Part 1-A Florida November 18; December 28, 29, 30, 1950; February 16, 17, 22, 1951. Testimony of DiLorenzo, Anthony, pp. 167-86, and DiLorenzo, Mrs. Anthony, pp.39-47.

a sign of respect or recognition of his position. Moreover, when Sam, much later in his adulthood, began going through family photo albums, he found a picture of Salvator and Rose up in the Catskill Mountains with members of the Five Families in New York. They were apparently on a hunting party, but they all had shotguns and wore suits. When he told us about the photo, Sam commented, "That's a bizarre thing. Who goes hunting in the mountains in suits?"

Sam also remembered an incident from very recent years. On a tour in which Scott Deitche was a part of the group, he started chatting with Sam and asked why Santo Jr. had been a pallbearer at Salvator's funeral. Deitche had not found anything about Salvator in his research; he thought the senior Zambon must have been really important to have had Santo as a pallbearer.

Sam's tale brings up the Italian Code of Silence. I asked him what the term meant. He said it is an "old-school term" from Sicily. "It basically means that our business is our business; we don't talk about our business." His grandfather adhered to the code. Sam realized that he had been raised with the code. To what degree John maintained that Code of Silence with Aunt Dot, we will never know. She certainly knew relationships from family dinners, social gatherings, and reading the newspapers. She may not have asked John about his activities and/or his family's activities. Whether or not she asked Rose about activities also is unknown.

We got further insight into male-female relationships from Sam. He told us that when he got married, one of his cousins pulled him aside and told him that he needed to make sure that he always treated his wife with respect. The theory handed down was that your wife was special; you needed to take care of her and provide for her—in effect, treat her with dignity. Any other women were to be kept out of sight.

I asked Sam how Aunt Dot would have have fit in with the Zambons and their extended family. He was sure that Aunt Dot, even though a divorced German Lutheran from Iowa, had been accepted. She had a pleasing personality and was easy to get along with, as Mary Bach had testified in the divorce hearing. She was John's wife, and he was respected. She and Rose got along well together. Therefore, the pallbearers at Aunt Dot's funeral were extended family who were there "because basically she was one of us, and she's family." Because she was John's wife, she would "be given all the dignity she deserved, and so you know they would show up at the funeral."

Another way in which John showed respect for Aunt Dot was that he went to the Lutheran church with her, according to Sam. Aunt Dot transferred from Hyde Park Presbyterian to St. Paul Lutheran in 1952. The Roll of Members from the church recorded that information, but no record says that John joined the church. The Record of Funerals recorded that Aunt Dot died on June 24, 1961, and was buried on June 27, 1961. Her membership record also says that she took communion on January 1, 1961, and on May 28, 1961. Finally, the church record of memorial gifts for May 27, 1962, says that Herbert L. and Olive A. Wagner gave money to the organ fund in memory of Aunt Dot. On the line just above their names, it is recorded that "Mr. John Zambon" gave money to the organ fund in memory of his wife.

Reflections

My search for Aunt Dot has ended. It has been a tale of research that evolved into a story with some surprising twists. Her first husband, on the face of all known information, had all the German and Lutheran and church credentials that made him seem like he would be a wonderful husband. But life choices made in the 1930s were based on formal and public social roles and rules. What spouses learned about each other in the privacy and intimacy of their marriage relationship could either bind them closer together or split them apart, as happened with Aunt Dot and August Gruhn. By contrast, Aunt Dot's second husband, on paper, appeared to be an unlikely match, based on family background, ethnic heritage, religion, and education. In the final analysis, the man who initially looked like an unlikely match proved to be a loving and respectful husband.

As I reflect on Aunt Dot's lost life, which has finally come together in bits and pieces over the last few years, I realize that her life choices exemplified a strong woman moving forward in the face of adversity. As an ordinary woman, a loyal wife, almost thirty years before the Women's Movement, she followed the cultural ideal for her generation. But when her initial choice of marriage did not turn out as anticipated, she showed courage and grit in the decisions she subsequently made. When discarded by her Lutheran minister husband, she did not waste her energy becoming bitter or playing the victim. She divorced him and began learning new skills so that she could teach. When money was tight and the road to finishing college seemed long and arduous, she did not give up. She kept putting one foot in front of the other—finishing one course and going on to the next. She never lost sight of her long-term goal.

When she wanted to marry John Zambon and her parents would not give her a wedding, she trusted her own judgment and risked a second marriage for love and companionship. Through it all, and despite her life being cruelly cut short, she remained true to the faith in which she had been reared. Often the life choices we make when we are young are not the same choices we would make when we are in our mature middle or older years. Clearly, for Aunt Dot, her Lutheran heritage had created a life-long meaning that she could not reject.

I hope her story will motivate readers to research other forgotten women who thrived before the 1960s. As Gerda Lerner wrote in her 1979 book, *The Majority Finds Its Past*, ". . . most women have remained anonymous in history." Obviously, centuries-old thinking does not do an about-face in a few decades.[41]

---

[41] Gerda Lerner, *The Majority Finds Its Past: Placing Women in History* (New York: Oxford University Press, 1979),172.

Epilogue

The Gift of Resilience
BY REV. DR. GARY WILKERSON

The story of Aunt Dot, Dorothy Louise Wagner, is one of overcoming adversity in a man's world. But it is more than that. In today's language, hers is a story of resilience. Her story gives us permission to ponder our own resilience.

Before reflecting further on Dorothy's life, it is important to declare that I believe God created all humans with resilience. From the onset of recorded history, human beings have shown great resilience in adapting to habitat, to other humans, to overcoming adversity, as well as to strengthening families and communities and nations. In fact, I believe resilience is a part of the fabric of being human. I believe resilience is a gift from God. God's gift lived strong in Dorothy.

She was raised in a loving, faith-filled home, in a small city, in an era that bred a sense of safety among its children. That sense of safety and of being loved was the petri dish of her resilience. In addition, Dorothy had a personal bed-rock of faith that forged the forward movement of her life. A bad marriage did not grind her to a halt! Being far from family did not maroon her in self-pity. Rather, in her resilience, she found friends, pursued her education, discovered a passion for teaching deaf and hard-of-hearing children, and was gifted with a man who loved her, John Zambon. One consequence of resilience is wonder-filled surprises. Dorothy's life seems to have been blessed with wonder-filled surprises.

The gift of resilience is to all humans, male and female. I suggest that there is no human era when resilience cannot be found. It weaves through individuals, families, communities, and nations. It can be found in equal share with men and women. It evidences itself in different guises with each individual regardless of their gender. It may show in grand historic events or intimate personal events, such as Dorothy lived. The wonder of a gift of God is that we are continually surprised where, when, and how it shows up.

Examples of resilience abound in biblical history. People of God have suffered hardship, persecution, loss, and betrayal, as well as joy, deep fulfillment, and a life filled with love both from other humans and God. The Psalms reflect all of these behaviors, and show us evidence of humans exhibiting resilience. In Psalm 23 God lays before us the groundwork for this resilient journey:

> The Lord is my shepherd; I shall not want.
>
> He makes me lie down in green pastures. He leads me beside still waters.
>
> He restores my soul. He leads me in paths of righteousness for his name's sake.
>
> Even though I walk through the valley of the shadow of death, I will fear no evil, for you are with me; your rod and your staff, they comfort me.
>
> You prepare a table before me in the presence of my enemies; you anoint my head with oil; my cup overflows.
>
> Surely goodness and mercy shall follow me all the days of my life, and I shall dwell in the house of the Lord forever.[42]

Psalm 23 reminds us that God promises to be with us through all of life's unpredictable ups and downs, through near-death experiences, pursuit by enemies, and sheltering blessings. Psalm 23 points us to a future without end. This psalm is the quintessential expression of resilience, faith, and trust in God. Dorothy was raised in an era when these beliefs were preached, taught, trusted, and held dear.

The Apostle Paul may have been an example for Dorothy. He has certainly been for countless Christians throughout the centuries. Paul experienced remarkable joys and hardships during his life and ministry. Read his resilient words from 2 Corinthians 4:8-18:

> We are afflicted in every way, but not crushed; perplexed, but not driven to despair; persecuted, but not forsaken; struck down, but not destroyed; always carrying in the body the

---

[42] The Holy Bible, English Standard Version (ESV) (Wheaton, Illinois: Crossway, a publishing ministry of Good News Publishers, 2001).

death of Jesus, so that the life of Jesus may also be manifested in our bodies. For we who live are always being given over to death for Jesus' sake, so that the life of Jesus also may be manifested in our mortal flesh. So death is at work in us, but life in you. . . . So we do not lose heart. Though our outer self is wasting away, our inner self is being renewed day by day. For this light momentary affliction is preparing for us an eternal weight of glory beyond all comparison, as we look not to the things that are seen but to the things that are unseen. For the things that are seen are transient, but the things that are unseen are eternal.[43]

Dorothy did not "lose heart." Her bad marriage did not "crush" her. Her divorce did "not drive her to despair." Her cancer did not "destroy" her because she did carry the life of Jesus within her. "Life" was always at work in her, another evidence of God's gift to us all—resilience.

Betty Ford was a contemporary of Dorothy, a public figure who stood tall in her resilience. As First Lady, she was the first to talk publicly about breast cancer. It was a taboo subject through history until 1974. Following her radical mastectomy in September 1974, Betty Ford publicly talked about breast cancer.[44] Her disclosure gave permission to women in America and around the world to speak about and deal openly with their own breast cancers. She gave permission to women to exhibit resilience and strength.

Then in 1978 her family held an intervention to confront her addiction to alcohol, pain medications, and sedatives. She was admitted to Long Beach Naval Hospital where Secret Service protection was easier. Four years later, following treatment and ongoing sobriety, she and Leonard Firestone, also recovering from alcoholism, created The Betty Ford Center. Leonard was the former CEO of Firestone Tire, her neighbor and a personal friend of the Fords. In the fall of 1982, they opened The Betty Ford Center in Rancho Mirage, California, to acclaim! The Betty Ford Center was truly unique and treated people with addiction from all over the world.[45] Mrs. Ford's openness about her addiction and recovery gave women around the world permission to deal with this deadly disease. The Betty Ford Center was the first in the world to have women as one-half of its patient population. Betty Ford personified resilience.

---

[43] Ibid.
[44] En.wikipedia.org/wiki/Betty_Ford.
[45] Ibid.

Let me share the story of another person I knew, for whom resilience seemed to have died but then returned in a remarkable manner. We will call him Albert. Albert (not his real name) was a patient assigned to me at The Betty Ford Center. I was one of the original staff when The Betty Ford Center first opened in October 1982. Eventually I became Director of the Inpatient Program. During Albert's time I was a case manager. He sat in my office, a man in his late 60s but looked fifteen years older. He was a gentle man, short, a cuddly-bear kind of man. He looked like everybody's favorite grandpa. I liked him instantly.

Outside my office window was a spectacular view of the pond and grounds of The Betty Ford Center property and the nearby San Bernadino mountains. Everyone who came into my office commented on the amazingly beautiful view! Albert didn't even notice. He just sat staring at the floor. He was slowly shaking his head back and forth, as if saying, "No! No! I can't believe this!" Immediately tears ran down his cheeks and great sobs racked his body. I let him cry. He needed to cry. He needed to scream out in anguish, and he did. His outcry startled me! His pain was so great, and so contagious, that tears came into my eyes, as well. I sat there watching and waiting, reflecting.

Albert was a nationally known and respected clergyman and leader in his church denomination. He had co-founded a well-known church college in Texas, had written books, been loved and respected by tens of thousands. He was currently the president of a prestigious, nationally-known church college in Southern California. Adding to his great shame, his denomination was one that not only frowned on drinking, it forbade it!

Now he sat in my office on a beautifully clear day, with a breath-taking view of the grounds and mountains, a patient at The Betty Ford Center, seemingly oblivious to his surroundings. What had happened, Albert? His life had turned to ashes; his spirit was near death; his resilience barely an ember. His sobs of shame and grief seemed endless.

As he continued to sob, I thought about how he came to be my patient. At The Betty Ford Center, patients were normally assigned to counselors in random order, but Albert had been especially assigned to me. He was a close friend of former President and Mrs. Ford. Mrs. Ford didn't normally interfere in patient care issues, but she had asked that I be Albert's counselor. As a fellow clergy member, she thought Albert might respond to me.

But, why the special treatment?

We had had clergy as patients before. That called for no special treatment. He had immense shame over his drinking. That was typical but called for no special treatment. He didn't understand the disease of alcoholism. That was typical but called for no special treatment. His denomination condemned alcoholism. That was sad and only too typical. But all of that didn't call for special treatment. We were all trained to deal with such issues. So what was it?

As great as his shame was over his drinking, it couldn't begin to describe the horror he now felt for the event that had brought him into treatment. The car accident! The accident created banner headline news that screamed out in Los Angeles and much of the country:

TWO WOMEN KILLED ON PACIFIC COAST HIGHWAY—
COLLEGE PRESIDENT RESPONSIBLE …

DRUNK CHURCH LEADER REAR ENDS CAR—
KILLING TWO WOMEN …

LOCAL UNIVERSITY MORTIFIED BY DRUNKEN PRESIDENT—
TWO WOMEN KILLED …

Albert, this loveable, elflike grandfather, in an alcoholic blackout had killed two women while driving! He didn't even remember the accident. He carried a manila file folder filled with newspaper articles about the accident. *They* were his memory. I had read through the articles before our meeting that day, so I was aware of the source of his universe-filling shame. Albert's life and spirit had turned to ashes. Even though his resilience was a mere flicker, he did agree to come to The Betty Ford Center for treatment of his alcoholism.

Saddest of all was his belief that God was a God of judgment and punishment. He had no concept of a God of grace. Can you imagine a life in which God has no compassion, no understanding, no mercy? That was Albert's God! No wonder he was terrified in his shame and grief.

It was as if Albert, this great churchman in his denomination, had not heard major passages in the Bible—the ones that tell of God's grace, understanding, compassion, and mercy, in spite of our brokenness, our sin. It was like he missed the Jesus who sat with sinners; who offered living water to a Samaritan woman and broke bread with the broken of the world. He missed the Jesus who breathed life into the ashes of our broken lives. Because of the event, God's gift of resilience to Albert was a dim, smoldering ember.

During his month-long stay in treatment, Albert began to hear and believe those great Bible passages—the ones that people thirsting for God need, the ones that heal our broken spirits, the ones that fan the flames of our resilience, the ones that give mercy and grace in our time of need.

Albert, "Jesus came while we were yet sinners" (Romans 5:8).

Albert, "Nothing can separate us from the love of God. Nothing!" (Romans 8:38-39).

Albert, "All who are without sin should throw the first stone" (John 8:7).

Albert, "Thus says the Lord, who created you, who formed you, do not fear, for I have redeemed you; I have called you by name, Albert, you are mine.

When you pass through the waters, I will be with you; and through the rivers, they shall not overwhelm you; when you walk through fire you shall not be burned, and the flame shall not consume you. For I am the Lord your God, Albert, I give Egypt as your ransom, Ethiopia and Seba in exchange for you. Because you are precious in my sight, and honored, and I love you (Isaiah 43:1-4a).

The resilient spirit seems to have an inner ear and an inner heart that can respond to words and acts that fan the flames of the near-dead embers of one's life. Gradually, life was breathed into the ashes of Albert's life and resilience. Grace gently began to touch and heal Albert's heart and spirit. He began to believe that *his disease* was evil, *he* wasn't. Jesus began to fill Albert's soul with life-giving mercy toward himself.

He wrote letters to the families of the women he had killed, knowing that nothing could bring them back. But he pledged to publicly fight the disease that had consumed him and destroyed them. After treatment he helped to change the perception of alcoholism in his denomination. Resilience evidences itself in behavior that matches one's words.

We see resilience in communities as well as individuals. Whole groups of people, tribes, regions, countries have often experienced such destruction or uprootedness as to seem destroyed. In 586 B.C.E. the capital city of the Jews, Jerusalem, was captured and destroyed by King Nebuchadnezzar, king of the Babylonian empire. This was an unthinkable shock to the Jews because God had led them to this land. God had promised faithfulness to them forever, and now the very city and Temple they had built to worship God was dismantled stone by stone! Their city was burned to the ground. Many Jews escaped but many were taken into exile in Babylon. How could this possibly happen?

The Babylonian Captivity was a defining moment in Jewish history. They went on for two generations feeling abandoned by God. The powerful lament of the Jews was captured in Psalm 137. They were so crushed they could no longer sing:

> By the waters of Babylon,
> there we sat down and wept
> when we remembered Zion.
> On the willows there
> we hung up our lyres.
> For there our captors
> required of us songs,
> and our tormentors, mirth, saying,
> "Sing us one of the songs of Zion!"
> How shall we sing the LORD's song in a foreign land?[46]

Their lamentations and lamentations throughout the Psalms have been portrayed as "the psalmist shaking one fist at God while holding God's hand with the other."[47]

Peoples throughout history have experienced such despair, have been uprooted from their homes and land; have lost hope and wondered where God was. In the twentieth century, hopelessness seemed to rule for a time. During World War II, six million Jews were exterminated by the Nazi regime. Secret concentration camps in Europe became, not just the modern-day Babylonian exile, but sites where enormous ovens were built to exterminate innocent Jews. A few survived. Viktor Frankl, an Austrian neurologist, psychiatrist, and author, was one of the lucky few. In his 1946 seminal book, *Man's Search for Meaning*,[48] he famously wrote, "If there is meaning in life at all, then there must be meaning in suffering."[49] He tells a poignant story of the men who walked through the huts in his concentration camp:

> We who lived in concentration camps can remember the men who walked through the huts comforting others, giving away their last piece of bread. They may have been few in number, but they offer sufficient proof that everything can be taken from a man but one thing: the last of the human

---

[46] The Holy Bible (ESV).
[47] Kathryn Schifferdecker, lecture series at Holden Village, July 30-Aug.3, 2018.
[48] Viktor Frankl, goodreads.com/author/quotes/2782. Viktor_E_Frankl.
[49] Ibid.

freedoms—to choose one's attitude in any given set of circumstances, to choose one's own way.[50]

Like the Jews at Babylon, the surviving Jews during the Holocaust discovered rebirth, life, and resilience in surprising ways. Predictably, the people discovered an old hope, a faith, an old strength and built a new future. The very next Psalm after the lament of Psalm 137 portrays this emergence of resilience for the Jews:

> Psalm 138
> I give you thanks, O LORD, with my whole heart;
> before the gods I sing your praise;
> I bow down toward your holy temple
> and give thanks to your name
> for your steadfast love and your faithfulness,
> for you have exalted above all things
> your name and your word.
> On the day I called, you answered me;
> my strength of soul you increased. . . .
> Though I walk in the midst of trouble,
> you preserve my life;
> you stretch out your hand against the wrath of my enemies,
> and your right hand delivers me.
> The LORD will fulfill his purpose for me;
> your steadfast love, O LORD, endures forever.[51]

Suffering often surprises us! One would think that a modern-day Christian congregation would be a safe place, filled with love, warmth, and acceptance—and they often are. Sadly, humans are complicated and do poorly when they exhibit being both sinners and saints. When the sinner side shows up, terrible pain and hurt can occur. Internal fighting erupts. People choose one side and reject the other side. The division may be over something inconsequential, like the color of the carpet in the sanctuary, or substantive, like the meaning of a biblical doctrine. The topic of the division hardly seems to matter when people are angry, disillusioned, and hurt.

I was the interim pastor at a dozen conflicted churches. Most of the places I served had experienced some sort of deep trauma. People took sides and mean-spiritedly accused each other of being wrong, stupid,

---

[50] Ibid.
[51] The Holy Bible (ESV).

selfish, and not following God. I found it fascinating that people in the church thought they could show behaviors that none of them would get away with in a public setting. During conflict in businesses, schools, communities, or government, no sane person would claim God was on their side. Church people do this all the time! Back in 1941-42, St. John's Lutheran in Des Moines had such a conflict; it ended in two associate pastors tendering their resignations. One was Dorothy's husband, August Gruhn.

Needless to say, during the interims I served, people were leaving and looking for other places to worship. Distrust ruled the day. In the process leading up to the conflict and explosion of emotions, people forgot basic concepts and became rigid in their stances, thus losing resilience, losing friendships, losing faith. Laughter died, and smiles disappeared. During each interim we talked about, studied, discussed, and confessed the importance of basic concepts within the church. For example: Do no harm. Know what you trust and believe. Remember history and the "big picture." Say and do what is "normal." Listen. Breathe deeply. Embrace time as a gift. Wait for laughter. Practice the Serenity Prayer.

The second day after starting an interim at a conflicted congregation I wrote a pastoral letter to the congregation. This is the letter that reflects the concepts listed above:

Dear Friends in Christ,

I begin my time with you humbly. Your church has been through a traumatic time. Your Senior Pastor has left after a relatively short period of service. Turmoil, conflict, divisions within the congregation, many questions and pain, have surrounded this event. I do not presume to say, "I understand how you feel." I do understand that there are as many strong feelings and opinions as there are people at your church. That is normal.

Such times are powerful, and sadly, not new in the history of God's people on earth. I believe that it is significant that I start my time with you during Advent. Advent is a time of anxious waiting, of wondering what new thing God is trying to have born. Nearly 2,000 years ago, as Mary and Joseph were waiting for the birth of their son, the Jews had been anxiously waiting for a new word from God for nearly 400 years. The people were hungry for light in their darkness. The people had settled into comfortable routines of life and worship. In their comfort, they thought they knew how God worked.

At such times, God always hears our cries and our needs. God gives us exactly what we need, except it often surprises us! The angel came to Mary and Joseph telling them God was giving them something very new. What a surprise! God gave them, and us, not only a new word, but also a word that breathed and walked. What a surprise! Nothing has been the same since! What a surprise!

Here is what I trust. I trust God to bring light into our darkness! I trust God to bring healing to our wounds! I trust God to bring unity to our divisions! I trust God to bring wholeness to our brokenness! And in the midst of it all, I trust God to surprise us again and again! . . .

Here is what I trust. I trust that when we humans stop long enough to breathe deeply, God may surprise us with something we could hardly dream of, like peace, comfort, love, joy, forgiveness . . . even unity.

Awaiting God's surprises with you,
Rev. Gary Wilkerson
Interim Senior Pastor[52]

For Christians, God has been modeling, acting out for us since the beginning what it means to be both diverse and unified. The body of Christ as a metaphor is a further evidence of both unity and diversity. They are a function of Creation itself. Therefore, I believe that we are expected to figure out how to do this in our churches, our relationships, our national and international policies. Unity and diversity are part of the fabric of Creation. It is how all of nature works together. It is how we are meant to work together, too, as people of the creation. It is not an option.

Suffering, pride, envy, jealousy, anger—the emotions that drive people apart—are not normal for God's intent for Creation. By contrast, the twelfth verse of John 14 holds one of the most awesome and challenging promises of Jesus in the Bible. He said, "You who believe in me will do the works that I do, and greater works will you do!"

---

[52] Gary Wilkerson pastoral letter, December 3, 2003.

I believe Jesus thought that what he did was not so incredible, so miraculous, so great. I believe Jesus thought that what he did was totally *normal*. Healings, walking on water, calming a storm, feeding the five thousand, raising people from the dead, changing water into wine are all *normal* events for God. The God who created sight, can give sight. That's normal! The God who created life, can give life back to dead things. That's normal! The God who created music, medicine, art, science, the knowledge of the universe, will give all of these to us. That's normal! For God, it is perfectly normal for God's people to create, mend, heal, come together, teach, inspire, change, guide, forgive, promise, and love! It is perfectly normal that we are resilient!

Resilience has been studied and written about a great deal recently. One hears of it referenced in individuals, in families, in politics, in the economy, in sports, in medicine, in dealing with all manner of stress and difficulty. We seem to be on a "Resilience band-wagon" these days. The tendency is to reference resilience to negative life experiences. However, more is being revealed about the positive strength of resilience. Synonyms for resilience give us words to look for in history and in the lives and writings of people. Consider doing research on words and phrases, such as, flexibility, durability, ability to last, strength, toughness, strength of character, adaptability, and buoyancy. These traits spring out of history in the lives of people from every continent and way of life. Check out the writings of such people as Martin Luther, Dietrich Bonhoeffer, Martin Luther King, Jr., Bishop Edmond Tutu, or the Dalai Lama. Resilience shouts from their lives and words!

Norman Garmezy, a developmental psychologist at the University of Minnesota, is noted for being the first to study resilience in a clinical setting, having studied thousands of children over forty years of research.[53] Garmezy's work

> opened the door to the study of *protective* factors: the elements of an individual's background or personality that could enable success despite the challenges they faced… his students and followers were able to identify elements that fell into two groups: individual, psychological factors and external, environmental factors, or disposition on the one hand and luck on the other.[54]

---

[53] Maria Konnikova, "How People Learn to Become Resilient," *The New Yorker* (February 11, 2016):1-7.
[54] Ibid., 3.

Emmy Werner, also a developmental psychologist, studied a group of 698 children for thirty-two years in Kauai, Hawaii. She published her findings in 1989 and had discovered similar findings to Garmezy. She stated that

> several elements predicted resilience. Some elements had to do with luck: a resilient child might have a strong bond with a supportive caregiver, parent, teacher, or other mentor-like figure. But another, quite large set of elements was psychological, and had to do with how the children responded to the environment. From a young age, resilient children tended to "meet the world on their own terms." They were autonomous and independent, would seek out new experiences, and had a "positive social orientation."[55]

Over my career as a clergy, seminary teacher, and therapist, I have observed countless examples of the power of resilience, people who "could enable success despite the challenges they faced."[56] It may seem surprising that a consistent place to discover resilience is during the dying process and grief. A person in the last stages of her fight with cancer declared, "Oh, I am not dying! I am living until I am dead!" Resilience.

In 2009 George A. Bonanno, Professor of Clinical Psychology and Chair of the Department of Counseling and Clinical Psychology at Columbia University's Teachers College, wrote a seminal book, *The Other Side of Sadness: What the New Science of Bereavement Tells Us About Life After Loss*.[57] He advanced the understanding of dying and grief by positing the results of research which concluded that resilience was what got people through the dying and grieving process.

Nearly fifty years earlier, Elizabeth Kubler-Ross taught of the six stages of death and dying: shock; denial; anger; bargaining; grieving; acceptance.[58] Bonanno teaches that resilience is the lubricant between the stages. He also suggests that one need not go through specific stages of dying and grief, rather, resilience itself seems to be the primary source of getting people through dying and grieving. He states:

> As I learned more about how people manage to withstand extremely aversive events, it became all the more apparent

---

[55] Ibid.
[56] Ibid., 2.
[57] George A. Bonanno, *The Other Side of Sadness: What the New Science of Bereavement Tells Us About Life After Loss* (New York: Basic Books, 2009).
[58] Elizabeth Kubler-Ross, *On Death and Dying* (New York: Scribner, 1969).

to me that humans are wired to survive. Not everybody manages well, but most of us do. And some of us, it seems can deal with just about anything. We adapt, we change gears, we smile and laugh and do what we need to do, we nurture our memories, we tell ourselves its not as bad as we thought, and before we know it, what once seemed bleak and bottomless has given way; the dark recedes and the sun once again peeks out from behind the clouds.[59]

Interestingly, humor seems to be a surprising component of resilience. Think of the many times a laugh has broken the tension of a sad or difficult moment. A smile at the right moment is shared with comfort and hope. It was something I watched for in all the pastoral interims I served, in therapy and in addiction treatment.

Bonanno lifts up the Mexican celebration of the Day of the Dead:

The air of lightheartedness and humor that pervades the Day of the Dead is in many ways typical of Mexican culture and its generally blithe attitude toward many otherwise serious subjects, including death. As the great Mexican poet Octavio Pas has observed, "The Mexican is familiar with death, jokes about it, caresses it, sleeps with it, celebrates it; it is one of his favorite toys and his most steadfast love."[60]

Humor. Resilience in one of its many guises. A person fighting addiction who experienced countless negative consequences of their addiction, stated through a smile, "Only God can save me from this disease. And God has made me alive. I am sober thirty-two years, so far. If you knew me before becoming sober, you'd say 'that is hilarious!'" Resilience. A couple being intentional to not let the three affairs of one destroy their marriage. "Our love for each other and God's love for us is stronger than this sinful betrayal! We are laughing together again!" They are still together five years later and more in love than ever.

Forgiveness. Another guise of resilience. In addiction, the inability to forgive leads back into one's addiction, a person will relapse. For all humans, the primary one to forgive is oneself! Once people have forgiven themselves for a hurt, a word, or a behavior, they have given themselves permission to forgive others, too. It is critical to note that Jesus forgave no one from the Cross. He said, "Father, forgive them for they don't know

---

[59] Bonanno, 81.
[60] Ibid, 161.

what they are doing!" (Luke 23:34) Jesus gave forgiveness of the others to God. Humans are typically terrible at forgiving, so we practice giving our need to forgive to God. The more we practice giving forgiveness to God, the more we are able to forgive, and the more resilient we become.

Persistence. Yet another guise of resilience. As I referenced earlier, my time working in chemical dependency treatment put me in contact with people from all walks of life. People came from all over the country and world for treatment. We had each patient write daily in a journal about how they were feeling, what they were learning, and how they might be changing. A pharmacist from a Southern state was admitted. He had "lost my house, my wife and kids, and my career because I stole and used drugs from my own pharmacy! I face jail time when I go home."[61] The first night he wrote one sentence in his journal, "I feel lower than a footprint!"[62] He was in treatment for six weeks, longer than most, due to the prolonged detoxification from his many drugs. Gradually, he engaged in treatment, rediscovered his strong, central-self, became a leader among the patients, and remained clean and sober after he returned home. He was persistent and forgave himself for his behaviors under the influence of addiction. Resilience.

What is resilience? There are many definitions. One of the broadest is from a research team headed by Helen Hermann, M.D.: "Fundamentally resilience is understood as referring to positive adaptation, or the ability to maintain or regain mental health, despite experiencing adversity."[63] Elaborating, the authors write:

> The findings of pioneering investigators indicate that intellectual function, cognitive flexibility, social attachment, positive self-concepts, emotional regulation, positive emotions, spirituality, active coping, hardiness, optimism, hope, resourcefulness, and adaptability are associated with resilience.[64]

Back to the heroine of this book. Dorothy exercised all of these characteristics. A steady constant for Dorothy was her faith.

Let's review some of the resilience-oriented writing around faith. Two leading theoreticians in faith development are Sharon Daloz Parks and James Fowler. Both have written extensively about faith as being

---
[61] The author's recollection of the patient's journal.
[62] Ibid.
[63] Helen Herrman, MD, et al., "What Is Resilience?" *La Revuie Canadienne de psychiatrie*, 56, no 5 (mai 2011): 258-265.
[64] Ibid., 260.

different from belief. Faith tends to be a core emotional reality whereas belief tends toward an intellectual construct:

> Faith development theory arises from the dialogue between developmental psychology and the study of religion. From this perspective, whether it is found in religious or secular forms, faith development theory invites us to recognize that faith is the activity of meaning-making in its most ultimate and intimate dimensions—finding pattern, order, and significance to our lives.[65]

More importantly for Parks and Fowler "faith is inherently relational. From its inception at a person's birth, when the most fundamental meanings about life are shaped within early caretaking relationships, convictional faith is forged with others."[66] Further, they asserted that "the role of the imagination helps create the master narratives that sustain faith."[67] A master narrative may say something like, "God is good, but life can be bad. In spite of the bad I can adapt, survive, and move forward in my life." The parents of my wife, Karen, practiced this sort of resilient faith.

Lee and Eleanor, a farm couple in eastern South Dakota, had five children, four boys and one girl. They farmed, had a large extended family, went to church, and lent a helping hand to others, especially during harvest. Over time, Eleanor developed a severe asthma and allergy problem that made her life on a farm untenable. During harvest she was unable to get out of bed, take care of the kids, cook, or perform her normal responsibilities on the farm. They were able to be persistent because their extended family and friends would come to the house and take care of her, the kids, and the household. The long harvest time became more tolerable due to the care and generosity of others. Resilience is nurtured within community.

Eventually, the doctors recommended a change of environment. Lee and Eleanor made a difficult decision to leave their friends, extended family, and church to move to Southern California to live in a dryer climate. The decision was all the more difficult because neither Lee nor Eleanor had jobs to go to in California, nor did they have much money. They left South Dakota in a small caravan: an old station wagon with five children, ages 1, 3, 5, 7, and 11; $500; and a farm truck filled with their possessions; plus a following car of relatives to help with the move.

---

[65] Gina O'Connell Higgins, *Resilient Adults: Overcoming a Cruel Past* (San Francisco: Josey-Bass Publishers, 1994), 172.
[66] Ibid., 175.
[67] Ibid., 177.

With humor they have described themselves as "the Grapes of Wrath-family." Faith, humor, persistence, and resilience were writ large!

Eleanor got a job on their first day in Southern California, and Lee got one a few days later. Eleanor's health took a dramatic turn for the better. Her asthma disappeared, and her allergies markedly lessened. God's gift of resilience surrounded them with surprising turns of events in their lives that moved them forward in unexpected ways, better than they could have planned. They were followed by the prayers of family and friends from South Dakota. There was great wisdom and resilience in the prayers that surrounded them.

The Serenity Prayer is a premier prayer that has followed and surrounded people for decades: *"God grant me the Serenity to accept the things I cannot change; the Courage to change the things I can; and the Wisdom to know the difference."* Basically, it tells us that I can change nothing else in the world, including people, circumstances, and history. I can only change myself. God give me the wisdom to remember this and act accordingly. People in all manner of recovery groups depend upon this brilliant prayer, written by Reinhold Niebuhr. He was an American Reformed theologian, ethicist, commentator on public and political affairs, and professor at Union Theological Seminary, New York.

The original version by Niebhur was longer and more revealing of resilience with an accompanying faith. He used the prayer in a sermon he preached in Massachusetts in 1934:

> God, give us grace to accept with serenity
> the things that cannot be changed,
> Courage to change the things
> which should be changed,
> and the Wisdom to distinguish
> the one from the other.
>
> Living one day at a time,
> Enjoying one moment at a time,
> Accepting hardship as a pathway to peace,
> Taking, as Jesus did,
> This sinful world as it is,
> Not as I would have it,
> Trusting that You will make all things right,
> If I surrender to Your will,

So that I may be reasonably happy in this life,
And supremely happy with You forever in the next.[68]

People who practice The Serenity Prayer grow more and more resilient. A young woman, Rose (not her real name), was an assistant counselor with me at The Betty Ford Center. I was the only male counselor in the Women's Building when we first opened. She was my assistant in group therapy and helped in managing my caseload. Rose had run away from home when she was 16 to get away from the physical and sexual abuse by her father and brothers. They were all drug- and alcohol-addicted, including Rose. She got clean and sober at the age of 18 while living on the street. When she started at The Betty Ford Center, she was ten years clean and sober, had a son, was a role model of sobriety to others, was street-tough, and was thoughtfully gentle. Rose practiced the Serenity Prayer in all of her life. Rose was resilience with skin on. So was Dorothy! Her life choices exemplified the wisdom in the Serenity Prayer.

Niebuhr's prayer sprang out of his understanding of the Bible. The Bible is the story of God with God's people. As God's people we show startling weakness and remarkable strength. The Bible shows God's faithfulness, even in the face of our betrayal and faithlessness. God is the stable one, the rock, the anchor, the bedrock of all things. While we, God's people, are portrayed as both sinners and saints.

This was the trusted air that Dorothy breathed as a child raised in the Lutheran church in Iowa. She breathed this air as a newly-married woman. She breathed this air as a mature working woman who married the love of her life. Breathing this air nourished her resilience, a gift from God, picked her up and strengthened her as life unfolded.

As you reflect on the stories of Dorothy, of Betty Ford, of Albert, of the lamentations of the Israelites, of the concentration camp survivors, of Lee and Eleanor, of Rose—look for the gift of resilience in your life. Watch for wonder-filled surprises! And practice the Serenity Prayer!

---

[68] Reinhold Niebuhr, Complete, unabridged, original version, skdesigns.com/internet/articles/prose/niebhur/serenity_prayer/

A Brief Guide To Research Strategies & Sources
BY KIMBERLY TUCKER

If you enjoyed this book, you might be considering how to begin researching your own family. The simplest and best way to get started is to start with yourself and work your way back to your parents, grandparents, and great-grandparents on Family Search (free) and or Ancestry.com (at a cost). Build what you know of your tree and then look for existing records for the individuals about whom you know little or nothing.

In the classes I've taught, I always suggest checking the Family Search Wiki. It is an invaluable free resource that is updated continuously. It can show you where to look for records in almost any geographic location around the world. The information is broken down into categories of available record collections by time span, so you know if the records you seek even exist and whether or not they are available online.

If the records are not available online and are not in a repository near where you live, you can contact libraries and historical societies in distant areas for assistance. Sometimes there will be a small charge for staff time as well as for copies and postage. Offer to pay costs up front; be polite and patient, but persistent. Genealogy research requires strong problem-solving skills and resourcefulness. Think of yourself as Columbo or Miss Marple.

Often, knowing where to look and getting started is the hardest part of your research. Start with a narrow question or questions. An example may be: When did Dorothy Wagner live in Tampa? An example of a research question that is too broad might be: Who are my ancestors? That's way too broad. Once you reach a point where you cannot get any further in the research, you could then hire a professional to help with "brick walls" or to go to a courthouse in a faraway locale, for example, to obtain records that can only be secured by a person on premises with an appropriate ID. If you decide to hire a professional genealogist, consult the following resources:

Association of Professional Genealogists (APG), www.apgen.org
Accredited Genealogist Researchers List http://www.icapgen.org

Board for Certification of Genealogists (BCG)
www.bcgcertification.org/associates/index.php
APG Code of Ethics https://www.apgen.org/ethics/index.html

The rates professional genealogists charge can vary widely, depending on where they live and other factors. I suggest contacting a few genealogists to get a range of quotes for your project.

However, if you want to continue on your own, the following is a list of guidelines and resources to help advance your search. It is by no means exhaustive. In addition, there are many more free and paid resources online and in print including webinars, podcasts, and books to help further your research and your education. A simple search with your favorite web browser will prove invaluable. To help make sure your work is accurate you can use established standards. I recommend spending some time getting to know the Genealogical Proof Standards by the Board for Certification of Genealogists.

Genealogical Proof Standards (GPS)

The Board for Certification of Genealogists states:

> The GPS overarches all of the documentation, research, and writing standards described in *Genealogy Standards*,[69] and is applied across the board in all genealogical research to measure the credibility of conclusions about ancestral identities, relationships, and life events. To reach a sound conclusion, we need to meet all five components of the GPS.
>
> 1. Reasonably exhaustive research.
> 2. Complete and accurate source citations.
> 3. Thorough analysis and correlation.
> 4. Resolution of conflicting evidence.
> 5. Soundly written conclusion based on the strongest evidence.

What Is Thorough Research?

- Make sure you have at least two items of evidence in agreement.
- Use primary sources, e.g. someone who witnessed the event. Technically, although you were at your birth, you are not a primary source for your birth because you cannot remember it. Your mother certainly would, however.

---

[69] Board for Certification of Genealogists, *Genealogy Standards*, 50th anniversary edition (Nashville, Tennessee: Ancestry, 2014).

- Find original records.
- Replace derivative sources, e.g., copies and transcriptions, with primary sources or original records whenever possible.
- Seek out all possible sources—leave no rock unturned.
- A *source* is "a person or thing from which something comes into being or is derived or obtained."[70] It can be a person, e.g., the "informant" (usually a close relative) and the doctor (who is also an informant) for a death record.
- A *record* is "an account, as of information or facts, set down especially in writing as a means of preserving knowledge."[71] A *record* serves as evidence and is also considered a *source*. A birth record is a source of evidence. Your mother and the doctor who helped deliver you are sources for the information contained in your birth record.

The research process should look something like this:

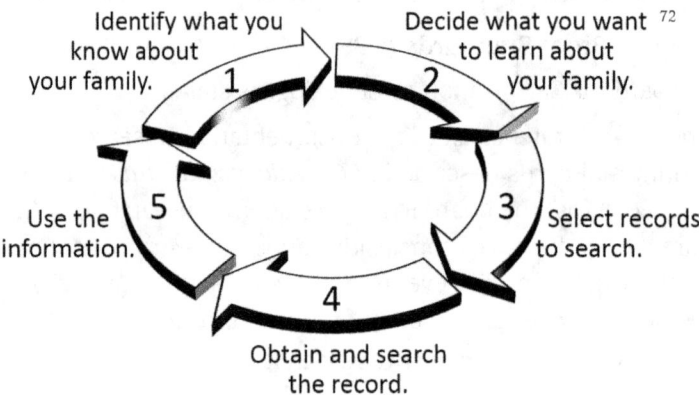[72]

A hypothesis is "a tentative explanation for an observation, phenomenon, or scientific problem that can be tested by further investigation."[73] If at first, you don't succeed, try to reject your hypothesis; this helps to eliminate a competing theory. Negative evidence can help to do this. Negative evidence is evidence which helps to disprove your hypothesis.

---

[70] American Heritage® Dictionary of the English Language, Fifth Edition. S.v. "source." Retrieved August 29, 2018, from https://www.thefreedictionary.com/source.

[71] American Heritage® Dictionary of the English Language, Fifth Edition. S.v. "record." Retrieved August 29, 2018, from https://www.thefreedictionary.com/record.

[72] FamilySearch Wiki contributors, "Research Process," FamilySearch Wiki. Retrieved August 29, 2018, from http://www.familysearch.org/wiki/en/index.php?title=Research_Process&oldid=3254483.

[73] *American Heritage® Dictionary of the English Language, Fifth Edition.* S.v. "hypothesis." Retrieved August 29, 2018, from https://www.thefreedictionary.com/hypothesis.

For example, while searching for Dot's residence during the years August Gruhn was stationed in various places in the U.S., we looked for her in the vicinity of where he was stationed, which seemed logical, but we learned, in some instances, she was not living in the same area or city.

What Is Most Likely To Be Accurate and Reliable Evidence?

- Eyewitness and participant (primary) information recorded *soon* after the event.
- Original sources. Alert—some records have errors possibly due to the person recording the information making a mistake or the informant providing misinformation. In addition, you may have to contend with torn or damaged records, altered photocopies or transcription errors. These issues can make the evidence less accurate and/or reliable.

Family Records

Start with what's near you. Go to your grandmother's attic if you can, or contact family members, and gather information such as:

- Family Bibles
- Letters, postcards, books
- Legal papers, receipts, bills
- Birth certificates, marriage, church and cemetery records, memorial cards
- Membership/club/organization records
- Old photographs, yearbooks, newspaper clippings, and other ephemera memorabilia. For more on ephemera see: http://www.ephemera-society.org.uk/articles/Ephemera_Genealogy.html and http://www.ephemera-society.org.uk/index.html
- Family group sheets, pedigree charts and other records from your ancestors

Relationship Terms

It can be confusing trying to determine who is who. Keeping track of third cousins twice removed can be a headache. If you have a big family, you know that your Aunt Linda is your cousin. She is old enough to be your aunt, and you think of her as your aunt, but know she is your cousin. Imagine going back a few generations with names of people who are new to you. For help with identifying relationship terms see: http://www.searchforancestors.com/utility/cousincalculator.html.

Research and Information Gathering

Your family records are in hand. Now what? You're ready to research. Determine which materials may answer your questions or test your hypotheses. Gather information and evidence. You can begin by looking for your ancestors/research subjects in the following public record groups: Census, Vital, Probate, and Land records.

U.S. and State Census Records
- wiki.familysearch.org—US census online
- www.familysearch.org
- www.archive.org/details/us_census
- www.census-online.com/links/
- www.ancestry.com
- http://www.heritagequestonline.com—at public libraries

State Census records were usually taken every five years and can help fill in gaps in your timeline.

Vital Records
- Vital records are birth, marriage and death records. You can start your search here:
- wiki.familysearch.org
- www.vitalchek.com
- www.familysearch.org
- www.ancestry.com

You can also order directly from your state or local office.

Some Substitutes for Vital Records: If you cannot find a vital record for your ancestor, try:
- Newspapers
- Church records
- Christening and burial records
- Tombstone & sexton records
- Funeral home records
- Obituaries
- Social Security Death Index
- School records
- Military records

Probate Records

Probate records often include wills, estate inventories, appointments of executors or administrators, petitions for guardianship of minor children, lists of heirs, and lists of debts.

Probate terms:

Testate—the deceased left a valid will

Intestate—the deceased did not leave a valid will

Testator—the deceased person who leaves the will

Executor (Executrix)—the person who executes the will in testate probate.

Administrator (Administratix)—the person appointed by the court to dispose of an intestate estate.

How do you find probate records?

- wiki.familysearch.org
- Family History Library Catalog
- www.ancestry.com
- www.familysearch.org

Land Records

Land case entry files can contain a wealth of genealogical and legal information. Depending upon the type and time period of the land entry, the case file may yield only a few facts already known to the researcher or it may present new insights about ancestors, family history, title, and land use issues. For example, the records may attest to one's age, place of birth, citizenship, military service, literacy, and economic status, and may even include similar information about family members. But even the smallest case files can establish locations of land ownership or settlement and dates essential to utilize other resources at The U.S. National Archives and Records Administration (NARA), such as census, court, and military service and pension records.[74]

Check the Bureau of Land Management (BLM), General Land Office (GLO) web site: www.glorecords.blm.gov. Their collection includes: land patents, survey plats and field notes, land status records, control document index records, tract books, and a land catalog.

---

[74] Archives.gov, "Land Records: Introduction to Links and Resources on Land Entry Case Files and Related Records." Retrieved August 29, 2018, from https://www.archives.gov/research/land.

You may have ancestors who lived near a border of a county so you will want to check the land records at the courthouse or property appraiser's website (for newer records) to determine if the records you seek could be in a neighboring county.

Military Records

If the person you are researching has served in the military, these collections may be helpful to you. Remember, as with all records, these records are not necessarily free of errors:

- Revolutionary War Pensions and Bounty Land Warrants—http://persi.heritagequestonline.com/hqoweb/library/do/revwar
- Civil War Soldiers and Sailors—www.itd.nps.gov/cwss
- World War I Draft Registration Card Index—http://content.ancestry.com/iexec/?htx = List&dbid = 6482&offerid = 0%3a7858%3a0
- World War II Enlistment—www.archives.gov
- World War II Bonus Case File and other military records—www.ancestry.com
- NARA—https://www.archives.gov
- Fold3.com

Other Useful Public Websites and Records:

Libraries & Archives

- Cyndi's List of Genealogy Sites on the Internet—www.cyndislist.com
- WorldCat—two billion items available through a library—www.worldcat.org
- USGenWeb (state & county vital & census records)—www.usgenweb.org/states/index.shtml
- BYU Family History Archive—www.lib.byu.edu/fhc
- NARA—http://www.archives.gov/genealogy/index.html
- Public Libraries so you can request obituaries—www.publiclibraries.com

Check the local library(ies) and historical societies where the person/s you are researching lived.

Tax Lists

Cornelius Carroll states in his book, *The Beginner's Guide to Using Tax Lists*:

> Taxes have been imposed by governments for many reasons and on many things. The records are diverse and you'll find

varying degrees of detail included. Taxes on land may include details on property owned, whereas a poll tax may only include a name, date, and location. In addition, while the items being taxed may be similar, the content of tax records may also vary from place to place.[75]

Cornelius Carroll goes on to note:

Tax lists are one of the most valuable, but most neglected sources of genealogical information. They cannot only be used to trace migration and determine the taxable property of ancestors, but they are also important because they can be used to prove parentage when no other records are available. There are also many other uses which many genealogists and historians do not suspect.[76]

Court records

We were able to get all of the files from Dot's divorce from the local courthouse. I went to the courthouse several times, developed a rapport with the employee who could help me and had to be patient. In some cases, it takes time and persistence. Courthouse employees had to dig through the archives in another building to obtain these records for us. We paid the standard fee they charged everyone else for copies, but the employees went the extra mile to help us.

Newspapers

One of my favorite sources for newspapers online is Newspapers.com ($). Others include GenealogyBank.com ($) and Fulton Postcards http://fultonhistory.com/Fulton.html (free). Several other online newspaper websites exist—some are free; some are not. Also, in many cases, you can still go to your local library and look at newspapers on microfilm or microfiche.

Passenger lists

If you are looking for your immigrant ancestor, you will want to check passenger lists:

- NARA: https://www.archives.gov/research/immigration
- Castle Garden—covers people immigrating/emigrating between the years 1830-1892 http://www.castlegarden.org/

---

[75] Ancestry.com, "Tax Lists." Retrieved August 29, 2018, from https://search.ancestry.com/search/category.aspx?cat=142
[76] Cornelius Carroll, *The Beginner's Guide to Using Tax Lists* (Baltimore: Clearfield Co.,1997).

- Ellis Island covers people immigrating/emigrating between the years 1892—1924 https://www.libertyellisfoundation.org/
- Various other ports of entry include Boston, Galveston, Philadelphia and New Orleans. Steve Morse's 1 Step Database can help you locate these files.
- www.jewishgen.org/databases/EIDB/ellisgold.html?firstkind = starts&FNM = &lastkind = starts&LNM =
- Ancestry.com
- FamilySearch.org

Passports and passport applications—https://www.archives.gov/research/passport

According to NARA:
> Foreign travel in the nineteenth century was much more frequent than one might expect. Overseas travelers included businessmen, the middle class, and naturalized U.S. citizens who returned to their homelands to visit relatives. For example, statistics show that the State Department issued 130,360 passports between 1810 and 1873, more than 369,844 between 1877 and 1909, and more than 1,184,085 between 1912 and 1925. It is unknown how many American citizens traveled abroad with passports issued by state or judicial authorities prior to 1856 or without any passport prior to 1918.[77]

Naturalization records

If you have foreign-born ancestors you will want to find their naturalization record. https://www.archives.gov/research/naturalization

School records

If your ancestor attended a school or university where the records are still available, it is well worth your while to request these records. They can give you a glimpse into courses taken, grades, costs, etc. For women, these records may be some of the few that exist. Contact the Registrar's Office for university transcripts. Special collections or the main library may also be helpful for your search. They can tell you how to use their proprietary databases (if they have them) and tell you which records they have that may be useful to you including yearbooks and campus publications.

---

[77] Archives.gov, "Passport Applications." Retrieved August 29, 2018, from https://www.archives.gov/research/passport.

Employment records

If employment records still exist for your ancestor, they can tell you quite a bit. In our case, Dot's file from the school district gave us her statement of teaching philosophy, one of only three short pieces of writing in her own words, that we were able to find. It also included her letters of recommendation, which gave us some insight into her character and abilities. Obtaining these records required us to provide a copy of Ann's driver's license and a bit of tenacity. In this case, I had to go in person to obtain the records.

Biographies

You may or may not be surprised to learn you had a governor in the family or someone of some influence. If so, check online and in libraries to see if you can find a biography for them—www.worldcat.org is a great place to start.

Histories

Local histories for the place where your ancestors lived can help put their lives in context.

Directories
- Find living people—www.peoplefinders.com
- Whitepages.com
- Anywho.com

Gazetteers

A gazetteer is a geographical dictionary or directory, an important reference for information about places and place names (see: toponomy), used in conjunction with a map or a full atlas. It typically contains information concerning the geographical makeup of a country, region, or continent as well as the social statistics and physical features, such as mountains, waterways, or roads.[78]

USGS geographic names query
- http://geonames.usgs.gov/pls/gnispublic/f?p = 154:1:3749245162408512
- https://www.census.gov/geo/maps-data/data/gazetteer.html
- http://guides.library.ucla.edu/c.php?g = 180224&p = 1190956#s-lg-box-3578181

---

[78] Wikipedia contributors, "Gazetteer," Wikipedia, The Free Encyclopedia. Retrieved August 29, 2018, from https://en.wikipedia.org/w/index.php?title = Gazetteer&oldid = 856390650.

Maps
- MapQuest—www.mapquest.com
- Google Maps—www.maps.google.com/ road maps and satellite views
- Sanborn Maps—https://www.loc.gov/collections/sanborn-maps/

Periodicals
Heritage Quest: PERSI—http://persi.heritagequestonline.com/hqoweb/library/do/persi

Cemetery Records
- USGenWeb Tombstone Project—http://www.usgw-tombstones.org/
- Find a Grave http://www.findagrave.com/
- Cemetery Records Online www.interment.net
- Billiongraves.com

Genealogy is a complex field of study and profession that is continuing to evolve. I've endeavored to give you some essential resources to begin your research, but there is always much more to learn. One must commit to lifelong learning to succeed as a genealogist. If you have started your research and would like to pursue a formal education to become a professional genealogist, start here:

https://www.apgen.org/articles/ready.html[79]

https://www.ngsgenealogy.org/cs/home[80]

Many genealogists are self-taught. The BCG recommends these books, journals, articles, and blogs:

https://bcgcertification.org/learning/reading/[81]

According to APG, you can also earn an advanced degree in genealogy from:

Boston University, Brigham Young University, International Society for British Genealogy and Family History, National Institute for Genealogical Studies, National Institute on Genealogical Research, Regional In-depth Genealogical Studies

---

[79] Apgen.org, "Becoming a Professional." Retrieved August 29, 2018, from https://www.apgen.org/articles/ready.html.

[80] Elizabeth Shown Mills, editor, *Professional Genealogy: A Manual for Researchers, Writers, Editors, Lecturers, and Librarians* (Baltimore: Genealogical Publishing Company, 2008).

[81] Thomas W. Jones, *Mastering Genealogical Proof* (Arlington, Virginia: National Genealogical Society, 2013).

Alliance, Salt Lake Institute of Genealogy, Institute of Genealogy and Historical Research, and the University of Washington Genealogy and Family History Certificate Program. Your local community college may have a family history program as well.[82]

Several free and paid webinars and other educational resources are available online. These resources are always changing and growing, so it helps to do a little digging online from time to time to keep your finger on the pulse and brush up on your skills. The process of discovery is gratifying and exciting. Happy hunting!

---

[82] Arlene Eakle and Johni Cerny, *The Source: A Guidebook of American Genealogy* (Salt Lake City: Ancestry Publications, 1984).

Dot's funeral folder.

About the Authors

Ann Wagner spent her teaching career at St. Olaf College, where she holds the rank of Professor Emerita of Dance. Although specializing in dance history, she also taught Introduction to Women's Studies several semesters.

Her combined interests in dance, history, gender roles and attitudes of the Protestant ministry in America all came together in her book, *Adversaries of Dance: From the Puritans to the Present* (University of Illinois Press, 1997). This book is currently held in 525 libraries around the world, including the British Library. She received a National Endowment for the Humanities Fellowship for College Teachers to write an initial draft of the book.

In retirement, Ann has been actively researching and writing family histories. In that role, she has continued more than a century-long connection of the Wagner family with Carthage College and with the Lutheran church. She lives in Burnsville, Minnesota, and can be contacted via wagnera@stolaf.edu.

In his varied career, **Gary Wilkerson** has served as a Lutheran church pastor, counselor, and seminary professor, as well as lecturer, consultant and retreat leader.

After several years as pastor of a Lutheran congregation in Simi Valley, California, he served for seven years on the initial staff of the Betty Ford Center, as case manager, supervisor and Director of the Inpatient Program.

Then, following four years as a parish pastor in Philadelphia, Gary began a doctoral program at Luther Seminary in St. Paul, Minnesota. Subsequently, he became a Visiting Professor for six years at the seminary.

In his final institutional role, he became Director of the Mt. Olivet Lutheran Church Counseling Center in Minneapolis, where he supervised a staff of six therapists and one administrative assistant, as well as carrying a full load of individual counseling, for nine years. In between these assignments, Gary served as a consultant, lecturer, retreat leader, and workshop facilitator for a variety of congregations.

Recently retired, he lives in Northfield, Minnesota, with his wife, who teaches voice at St. Olaf College. He can be contacted via gwilkerson001@luthersem.edu.

Kimberly Tucker has ten years experience in genealogy research. She has taught a class in beginning genealogy research at the University of South Florida as part of their Osher Lifelong Learning Institute. She is also a faculty member at the National Institute for Genealogical Studies, an affiliate of the Continuing Education Division of St. Michael's College in the University of Toronto.

Kimberly holds membership in several professional associations and has written a series of columns for the Association of Personal Historians about how to incorporate genealogical research into personal histories. As a longtime resident of Tampa, Florida, Kimberly specializes in local resources, but has research experience in a number of subject areas and geographical locales. Like Aunt Dot, Kimberly holds a bachelor's degree from the University of Tampa. She can be contacted via kimtucker@protonmail.com.